MEDIA BEYOND BORDERS: A SOUTH ASIAN PERSPECTIVE

EDITED BY V. RATNAMALA & SAYAN DEY

Contents

Preface

Globalization today can not be compared with Westernisation only. With the availability of multi-channel global television, non-Western culture is being equally imposed on people around the world. Just as western cultural programmes and Hollywood films are being consumed internationally, non-Western cultural programmes like Korean serials, Japanese Anime and bollywood films are being consumed universally. Significantly, the television industry in India is going global and local. We can call it as glocalization postulated by Roland Robertson. According to him, glocalization is the adaptation of global products to the local context and culture. Glocaliztion means that trends of homogenization and heterogenization exist side by side in this modern world. According to Robertson the use of the term glocalization means that it is local culture which give meaning to global influences, and that the two are therefore mutually dependent and facilitate each other. Now the Indian television is glocalized its content and programming style.

Media products play a significant role in the daily processes of transcultural communication. Media products are nothing but television series, YouTube clips, online readings, films and all the other kinds of media as we consume them. In the context of economy, media product referred as commodity. Here the term "media product" will be used as a generic term for all the various media contents and media texts related to transcultural communication. Here we are concerned about how we are making transcultural communication through these media products and the things we share through this transcultural communication. Due to the advancement of globalization and the increase of transcultural communication, it is very difficult to categorize the media representations based on territory.

This edited volume explores the potential of transnational media content in South Asia, particularly InThe goal of this edited collection is to bring together media scholars from around the country to discuss issues related to Asian media realities that transcend national borders. Specifically, India. In this curated collection, we will explore all aspects of international communication. A globalised modern media requires a range of approaches and disciplinary lenses, which are emphasised in these contributions. The collection is unique in that it discusses the influence of Turkish serials,

Japanese anime, and the Korean wave on India from both theoretical and practical perspectives.

Editors: Dr. V.Ratnamala & Dr. Sayan Dey

CHAPTER I

"Annyeonghaseyo!": Bringing Korean Culture to the World

Ujjaini Chakrabarty, PhD Scholar, Dept. of Mass Communication & Journalism, Tezpur University

Abstract

Relatively unknown until the late 1990s, the South Korean entertainment industry has emerged as the leading crowd puller in the recent times. The Second Korean Wave, or Hallyu 2.0 that began with the global hit *Boys Over Flowers* in 2009, has influenced cultures all over the world in many ways. While its significant presence in the fashion and beauty industry is conspicuous, the penetration of Korean Wave into the lifestyle of people also deserves scholarly attention. Apart from music and drama, Korean popular culture carried Korean cuisine onto the dining tables across the world. In India, children as young as 11 years can be heard saying *Kam-sa-ham-nida,* along with *dhanyavaad,shukriya,* and *thank you.* The Hallyu stars' worldwide popularity and their association with international artistes has also facilitated cultural globalization. So, what does the emergence of the Korean Wave mean for cultures globally?

The present paper thus, aims to revisit the concept of culture industry with reference to the second Korean Wave. A selection from amongst the most popular Korean dramas and music produced during this period will be chosen for analysis. The paper will further explore the reasons why in spite of the dark side of the Korean entertainment industry, charges against the creation of false beauty standards in people, and other criticisms, the influence of Korean pop culture cannot be underestimated, whose rising influence is steadily forging ahead to making South Korea a potential cultural superpower.

Keywords: Korean Wave, Hallyu 2.0, K-pop, K-drama, cultural globalisation, culture industry

Introduction

The penetration of globalization into most parts of the world during the last decade of the 20th century, made trade easier due to easing of restrictions on trade laws and tariffs, which facilitated rapid economic development in these places. However, this ease of transaction was not limited to consumer goods alone. The direction of the transnational exchange of cultural products, which was heavily skewed in favour of West in the preceding decades was now also being reversed. The entertainment industry of Asian countries like China, Japan, India and South Korea were now making their presence felt on the global stage. While Japanese and Indian films were already popular globally due to the works of auteur filmmakerslike Akira Kurosawa (known for films like Rashomon made in 1950) and Satyajit Ray (pioneer of the New Wave in Indian Cinema),Chinese actors like Bruce Lee, Jackie Chan, and Jet Lihad also reached Europe and North America through the English-dubbed versions of their films by the late 1980s,graduallymaking Chinese martial arts a rave in the West. The commercial and critical success of Ang Lee's *Crouching Tiger and Hidden Dragon* (2000)gave impetus to the production of Wuxia stories (part of the popular culture of China which tell the stories of ancient heroes) not only in films but also in dramas, whose popularity has only grown in the recent times. According to the report of Research on China's Internet Audiovisual Development in 2020, the Chinese television series *The Untamed* (released in 2019, based on the novel *Mo Dao Du Shi* by the author Mo Xiang Tong Xiu) starring amateur actors Xiao Zhan and Wang Yibo, was ranked first in the popularity index. The series had passed over 9.5 billion views in 2021, making it a global success.

Amidst these Asian giants though, South Korean entertainment industry gradually made its way into theneighbouring countries like Taiwan, Japan, Hong Kong, Philippines, Vietnam, Thailand, China, India and others. Relatively unknown until the early 90s, South Korean entertainment industry rose to prominence in the late 90s becoming the most important cultural product exported from Korea. The Korean cultural industry that was increasingly becoming popular came to be called 'Hallyu', a term which was coined by the Chinese media in 1998 to describe the sudden rise in popularity for Korea's popular culture amongst the Chinese youth. Today, the popularity of Korean entertainment has also brought Korean culture to the world. Along with the Korean drama and music, Korean cuisine, lifestyle, and beauty products have become a craze all over the world.

Most notably, Korean popular music has created a global fanbasedue to its catchy melodies, musical themes, elaborate dance, and music videos with artistic and bold visuals (Park, 2019). According to the 2018 report by Hyundai Research Institute (HRI), the boy band BTS alone generated

"4 trillion won ($3.54 billion) as economic value to the country per year and 1.42 trillion won ($1.26 billion) as added value per year" (ibid). In the same 2018 report, HRI also estimated that "BTS's ten-year economic impact will reach 56.2 trillion won ($49.8 billion)" (ibid). Korean music artistes are now collaborating with international musicians, enabling the creation of a cross-cultural blend of music styles,which have transcended linguistic barriers to reach the widest possible audience.Music video for "Gangnam Style", released in 2012 by Korean rapper and singer Psy, for instance, hit 3 billion views on YouTube in 2019, while the boy band BTS, launched in 2012, became the first K-pop band to top the US album charts and has more than 12 million subscribers on YouTube (as of 2019).Some of the K-pop bands now also have members from different countries (Jackson Wang of GOT7 from Hong Kong; Blackpink's Lisa from Thailand; Ailee from USA; Momo of Twice is Japanese; Yatou of Blackswan is from Senegal; SreyaLenka of India is yet to debut as the fifth member of the girl band Blackswan).

Even the superhero genre could not remain untouched by the Korean Wave. In the San Diego Comic-Con in July 2022, Marvel Comics announced the debut of its team of South Korean Superheroes and was named the Tiger Division. The five-issue series will be created by the writer Emily Kim and artist Crees Lee and will be released in November 2022. In 2014, Marvel the South Korean Actress Claudia Kim in *Avengers: Age of Ultron* in 2014. The Marvel Cinematic Universe has also cast another South Korean actor Park Seo-Joon for its upcoming movie that will be released in 2023.

In spite of the commercial and cultural success of the Korean Wave, the dark side of the South Korean entertainment industry, however, has not gone unnoticed. The grueling training process of artistes, continuous invasion of privacy, constant fan-wars between the followers of different artistes, trolling by anti-fans are some of the pressing concerns that have been raised by scholars and audience members in the past few years. The suicide of idols like Kim Jong Hyun in 2017 (band member of SHINee), Choi Jin-ri aka Sulli in 2019, and many others brought to light the mental pressure associated with becoming idols, whose actions are strictly watched by fans, anti-fans and especially their talent agencies. Apart from this, the constant reminder to look young and beautiful, with flawless skin affects the health of the idols who are reported to have gone through extreme diet to avoid being bullied on the social media, by fans and anti-fans alike.

In this present context, gaining an insight into the rise of the Korean entertainment industry, its influence on popular culture globally and its implication on the society, gains relevance.Thus, for the purpose of the present paper, some of the most famous Korean media products such as dramas, music, and artistes who contributed to the growth of the Korean Wave and turned it into a global phenomenon has been analysed through the perspective of the concept of culture industry, which was expounded by the Frankfurt School in the 1940s. These include the dramas *Winter Sonata* (2002), *Boys Over Flowers* (2009) and *Mr.Queen*(2020). Apart from Korean drama, Korean-pop, more commonly called as K-pop has also made ripples in the global pop music industry. Of the famous K-pop talents, the all-boy group BTS (BangtanSonyeondan or Bangtan Boys), the all-girl group Blackpink and the South Korean singer and rapper Park Jae-Sang, more famously known as Psy, will be used for the analysis.

History of Hallyu

The primary focus of the Korean Wave in the initial stages was on exporting television dramas to neighbouring nations like China and Japan; currently the export of Korean cultural productsincludes a wider range of Korean media and cultural products, such as Korean popular music films, online games, sports (sports players), and cosmetics. Even Korean cuisine and language have reached the USA, Europe and also the Middle East. When seen within the global context, Park (2019) observes that the Korean Wave phenomenon can be thought of as the creation of "a regional 'Asian' cultural manifestation against the erstwhile domination of Western culture." Indeed, the Korean Wave offers a platform for what KuanHsing Chen calls "Asia as method" in which "using Asia as an imaginary anchoring point can allow societies in Asia to become one another's reference points so that the understanding of the self can be transformed, and subjectivity rebuilt". However, even though the Korean phenomenon began in the mid-1990s, it took the academic community some time to realise the significance of the proliferation of Korean entertainment industry in the global cultural sphere. Only recently has there been a rising interest in Hallyu as a subject of study.

Lee Songjun (2015) has identified four stages of Hallyu scholarship. In the first stage, the growth and necessity of defining Hallyu and the popularity of pop content amongst Asians was studied. Until the beginning of the 21st century, there was sparsely any academic literature on the Korean popular culture; the only English-language literature on the topic was Yersu Kim's *Cultural Policy in the Republic of Korea*, which was commissioned by the UN in 1976. 'The strategic governmental effort did not disappoint, as Korean cultural content exports increased from $500 million in 2000-2002 to $800 million in 2004. Since then, Korean cultural exports rose exponentially, reaching $4.42 billion in 2010.

Songjun (5; 2015) states: "fans, scholars, entrepreneurs, and policymakers in Korea were altogether surprised, excited, and proud of the sudden explosion of Korean "low" cultures in adjacent countries, the Korean pop music craze in China in particular".

In the second stage, the endeavour was to "appropriate" the Hallyu Wave amidst the debate of cultural imperialism, reverse cultural imperialism and the shift in the flow of media content from the West. For decades after its independence in 1948, South Korea's major market was the West, especially USA. Through this trade route, American popular culture also reached South Korea. From the 1960s, Western media products, predominantly American, had spread to most parts of the world. Along with their movies, drama, and music, American culture was also making its presence felt in the more traditional societies, especially in Asia in countries like India, China, Korea and others. Park (2008) notes that after the advent of globalization in the 1990s, the flow of cultural products from the West to the East has witnessed drastic changes. The Asian media industry steadily made its foray into foreign lands where it made a market for themselves, bringing a large revenue from the overseas market. The beginning of the era of globalization also brought a change in the cultural policy of Korea. The cultural policy undertaken by the Korean government in the 1990s strived to be "democratic, neoliberal, globalist and remarkably state-driven". In his research on the role of the government in the growth of cultural industry in Korea, Kang Ah Park (5; 2008) states that the uniqueness in the trading of cultural products lies in the fact that their transaction is more flexible and faster, and that "there are fewer transactions, such as tariffs or customs law, than in any other types of trade". The governmental efforts at promoting Korean cultural content were met with success; it increased from $500 $500 million in 2000-2002 to $800 million in 2004, and has recorded exponential growth, reaching $4.42 billion in 2010 (Park, 2019). The modernization of Korea required the nation to be flexible, innovative, efficient, and fluid. The rapid development of the country and society has also made Koreans proud, confident, and diligent, motivating them to devote themselves to national and individual advancement. For instance, the 2019 enrollment rate of eligible students at South Korean Universities was 67.8 percent while, according to 2016 data compiled by the Organisation for Economic Co-operation and Development (OECD), South Korea has "longer working hours than any other developed country: an average 2,069 hours per year, per worker."

By the third stage of Hallyu scholarship, the popularity of Korean Wave facilitated the study of Hallyu as a "dynamic inter-Asian cultural flow". This is in spite of the fact that just 65years ago Korea was a war-devastated country that depended upon relief supplies from more developed nations of the world. South Korea's per capita GDP, for instance, was $156 in 1969 but rose to $36,776 in 2018. This explosive economic growth was largely facilitated by "compressed modernity", a form and condition for modernization where cultural, social, political, and economic changes take place in an extremely compressed manner in terms of both space and time, leading to "the construction and reconstruction of a highly complex and fluid social system" (Park, 2019).Youna Kim in her introduction to *The Korean Wave: Korean Media Go Global* notes, Korea's export of popular media culture was initiated by the government at the time of the 1997 Asian financial crisis as "a new economic initiative, one of the major sources of foreign revenue vital for the country's economic survival and advancement." Park (2008) observes that the popularity of Korean Wave has brought a sense of "cultural pride" that was hitherto missing in Korea. Park further agrees with the neo-liberal view that the popularity of the Korean Wave can be conceived as an opportunity to "advance and foster the cultural industry". This growth of the Korean entertainment industry was also supported as well as promoted by the Korean government. All these social, cultural, and national elements and characteristics of Korea have provided the foundation for the nation to establish itself as a leader in the global media and technological landscape (Park, 2019).

Park (2019) argues that the rise of the Korean Wave across the globe allows Korea to become the very reference and anchoring point for not only the nations within Asia but also those outside Asia. Through the understanding of the Korean Wave, Korea's own subjectivity can be rebuilt) from the Morning Calm to the global cultural and techno hub), the pan-Asian identity can be restructured through the lens of "pop Asianism" and understanding of the West and globalization as a Western cultural force can be de-Westernised and de-parochialised.'

In the fourth stage, Hallyu's domestic as global presence was studied vis-à-vis the growth of internet. "Korea, with the world's second-fastest average mobile internet speeds and the highest rate of smartphone ownership, is one of the leading nations in Asia bringing about these very "trend-setting innovations" in a wide range of media and technology, produced and consumed inside and outside the country.

Scholars engaged in the study of Hallyu remark that another important factor that has contributed to the success of the Korean Wave is the"emotional relevance and resonance that Korean popular culture seems to evoke in the minds of audiences around the world" (Park, 2019; Kim 2019). The South Asian audience was drawn to the Korean dramas because of commonality in cultures, values, aesthetics, morality, especially family relations which are founded on the Confucian philosophy. The dramas and movies produced in the early 2000s had traditional themes. Since the expansion of the market for Korean cultural products beyond its neighbours, a change can be observed in the themes, content and also the portrayal of characters who face the same struggles as others

What is important to note here is that empathetic emotion, which, according to Patrick Hogan, verbal art universally aims to evoke in the minds of the audiences, can be triggered either by the situational particularity or group identity. The universal human capacity to feel empathetic emotions for others (including for fictional characters) allows the overseas audiences of Korean popular cultural products to feel for and relate to what they read, watch, or listen to regardless of their own widely different cultural, regional, ethnic, and linguistic backgrounds (Park, 2019). The content of Korean dramas and movies are based on the lives of average people. While the concept of 'rich falls in love with the poor' theme still persists, it co-exists with the stories of characters that have other regular jobs, like Ji Chang Wook's character of the owner of a convenience store in *Backstreet Rookie* (2020), or Park Min Young working in Korea's Meteorological Department in *Forecasting Love and Weather* (2022), and other such characters which have broken the trend of 'giving' stereotypical jobs and identities to people in the stories. What makes these stories endearing is also the fact that they are light-hearted, present a picture of 'this too shall pass' and most importantly, the dramas are broadcast for shorter periods, which are usually wrapped up in 16 or 20 episodes. The shorter broadcast period allows the production of more content which can be binge-watched, a concept which has become the hallmark of viewing experience on the OTT platforms. These features of the Korean entertainment industry are reminiscent of the discussion of the global cultural industry that was initiated in the 1940s by the Frankfurt School of Germany, which studied the production process of the media against the backdrop of its socio-cultural significance.

CULTURE INDUSTRY

During the 1930s, one of the important academic developments of the time was the founding of the Frankfurt School,which was associated with the Institute for Social Researchat the University of Frankfurt, founded by a scholar named Carl Grunberg in 1923. Due to the growth of Nazism andanti-semitic sentiments in the 1930s, the School was moved several times. In 1933, the Frankfurt School was moved to Geneva in 1933, wherefrom it was shifted to Columbia University in New York. Theodore Adorno, Max Horkheimer, Leo Lowenthal, Friedrich Pollock, Herbert Marcuse and later Jurgen Habermas, Axel Honnethwere few of the famous exponents of the Frankfurt School.

The scholars at the Frankfurt School wanted to make research supra-disciplinary, i.e., they tried to incorporate theoretical approaches from across disciplines and create a social theory based on Marx and Hegel, disciplines such as psychoanalysis and sociology. They used the basic concepts of Marxism such as alienation, commodification, etc., to study social relations in a capitalistic economy.

One of the important concepts associated with the Frankfurt School is that of the 'culture industry'. It was first used by Theodore Adorno and Max Horkheimer in their book *Dialectics of Enlightenment* (1947; Adorno 1975; Bernstein 2019). Originally, Horkheimer and Adorno has used the term "mass culture", but later replaced it with "culture industry" to exclude the (mis)interpretation that the term referred to the culture that spontaneously arises from the masses (Adorno 1975; Bernstein 2019). Historically this was the time when great advancements were being made in the technology used for the production and dissemination of media products. After the end of the Second World War, colonies had gained independence, politically, but had to rely on the more developed nations for their own development. Through this trade route, cultural products were also exchanged, which was dominated by the Western culture.

The Frankfurt School postulates thatlarge corporations industrialised and thereby monopolized the production not only of consumer goods but also of cultural products, which led to a decline in individual consciousness, leading people farther from real pleasure but closer to the'illusion' of the experience of real pleasure. In the view expounded in the concept of 'culture industry', the products of culture, like music, painting, film, literature, etc., are valued not because of their content or harmonious formation, but due to the economic benefit attached with the product.

According to Adorno (1975), culture industry integrates its consumers from above, forcing the spheres of 'high art' and 'low art' to coalesce which leads to the destruction of the seriousness of high art, and also crushes the spirit of low art by bringing it under the control of the same authorities it was created to rebel against. The consumer, then, is not the subject but the object of culture industry, that "the masses are not the measure but the ideology of the culture industry, even though the culture industry itself would scarcely exist without adapting to the masses. Adorno further states (1975)

Culture, in the true sense, did not simply accommodate itself to human beings, but it always simultaneously raised a protest against the petrified relations under which they lived, thereby honoring them. Insofar as culture becomes wholly assimilated to and integrated in those petrified relations, human beings are once more debased. Cultural entities typical of the culture industry are no longer also commodities, they are commodities through and through.

The present-day creation of cultural products is primarily driven by the motivation to earn maximum profit. However, Adorno (1975) concedes to the importance of culture industry as the predominant spirit of the times it is situated in, but at the same time cautions against accepting its effect seriously.Horkheimer and Adorno (1947) had identified a few basic strategies that were adopted by culture industries to reach the audience. These included, style, genre, formula, imitation and the star system. These characteristic features of the culture industry find resonance with the Korean phenomenon which relies heavily on the image of the idols, their global popularity and the creation of content that audiences all over the world can identify with. Remakes, spin-offs and sequels are also a part of the re-presenting the same content in different places with the expectation of repeating the success of the original content. For instance, the 2009 television series *Boys Over Flowers* was so popular in Korea that it catapulted actors Lee Min Ho, Kim Bum and others to instant stardom. Multiple remakes have been made of the same in different languages and in different countries, the recent one being the Thai production *F4 Thailand: Boys Over Flowers,* which was aired in 2021-2022, and starred Vachirawit Chivaree, TontawanTantivejakul among others. *Winter Sonata,* which was aired in

2002, had become extremely successful, especially in Japan. Apart from the story, the music of the drama was also very popular among the audience.

In 2021, the Korean costume drama *Mr.Queen* which tells the story of a modern-day chef who meets with an accident and time travels into the Joseon era, that too into the body of a royal lady, broke its personal record to become the fifth highest rated show in the history of tvN. After the success of the drama, two more spin-offs, *Mr.Queen: The Bamboo Forest* and *Mr. Queen: The Story* were made as the prequel to the original series.

As stated earlier, in spite of its success, the Korean entertainment industry has also been criticized for the creation of false beauty standards among people. "Lookism", a term used to refer to the attitude of privileging physical attractiveness, is especially widespread and deeply rooted in modern Korean society. The popularity of Korean pop music, drama, and film naturally leads to the increasing popularity of individual artists and performers, and the Korean Wave consumers' desire to look and dress like them.' The extreme lookism of Korean society leads to many severe problems, such as eating disorders and excessive bodybuilding and exercises, but has also contributed to the global spread of and aspirations for the Korean-lifestyle. The Korean beauty industry, for instance, is among the top 10 around the globe, with an estimated worth of over \$13.1 billion in sales in 2018 alone. The craze for 'Korean glass skin' can be observed on the beauty channels on YouTube, where any caption that reads Korean skin pulls in thousands of views, without consideration for the scientific proof for the efficacy of the beauty trend being promoted.

It is also notable that one out of two Koreans is regularly on a diet, rigorously controlling his or her daily food consumption. According to the 2015 survey by Nielsen Korea, conducted online with 3 million people from 60 different countries, 6 out of 10 Koreans answered that they thought themselves to overweight, marking higher (60 percent) than the global average of 49 percent. This is striking especially given that Korea has the lowest overweight rate among all OECD nations. The Koreans' concern over-weight can be witnesses from the fact that often the characters in the stories who refer to having only one meal a day to check their weight.

The obsession to look like K-pop idols is not a domestic occurrence. In 2021, a 26-year-old Vietnamese man underwent multiple plastic surgeries to look like K-pop idol. In June 2021, British social media influencer Oli London shared pictures on his social media accounts to show the surgeries he had undergone to look like the BTS-member Jimin.

In their analysis of culture industry, Adorno and Horkheimer remark that "culture has become openly, and defiantly, an industry obeying the same riles of production as any other producer of commodities." (Bernstein, 2019). The mass production of cultural products leads to the loss of individuality, thereby affecting the uniqueness of the artist and the art form. A common theme and format prevail. The Korean Wave phenomenon can also be seen to be undergoing the same turmoil where, in an effort to create and sustain its global image, Korean cultural products are becoming more international in their approach, losing touch with the "Korean" in Korean culture industry. The commercial success of the phenomenon has no doubt brought huge revenues for the country, but it has far-reaching implications for both the Korean society which is endeavoring to become global in the Western sense, and also on the audiences in the other countries who are adopting Korean culture as shown in the dramas, thereby retaining balance between the 'global' and the 'Korean', albeit on lands foreign to both.

Bibliography:

1. Adorno. T., Rabinbach A.G. (1975). *Culture Industry Reconsidered*. New German Critique. No.6. pp 12-19
2. Adorno. T. (2019). *The Culture Indsutry: Selected Essays on Mass Culture*. New York. Routledge.

_______ Bernstein, J.M. *Introduction*. pp 1-28.

1. Park, H. (2019). *Understanding Hallyu: The Korean Wave Through Literature, Webtoon, and Mukbang*. New York. Routledge
2. Lee, Hye-Kyung. (2019). *Cultural Policy in South Korea: Making a New Patron State*. New York. Routledge
3. Kim, Youna. (2019). *South Korean Popular Culture and North Korea*. New York. Routledge.
4. https://www.statista.com/statistics/316810/box-office-revenue-india/
5. https://www.marvel.com/articles/comics/sdcc-super-heroes-south-korea-tiger-division-1

CHAPTER II

Reflection of Mizo culture in Korean Series

Remruatkima, Guest faculty, Govt K.M High School, Aizawl, Mizoram

Introduction

Korean wave is blowing strongly in today world. Korean wave is blowing in the world of dance, music, serials and films.They are very popular in the field of drama/serials. These serials are translated into various language. In Mizoram, Korean dramas are popular among children, adults and the elderly. Film dubbing in Mizoram has started immediately, Korean serials have spread to Mizoram. Korean serial hits are being translated by translators. The translation of Korean dramas has sparked a lot of controversy, with many critics and those who have banned the translation.

The reason for this is that Korean culture has destroyed Mizo's and the domestic violence, bad language and fighting that we see in K Drama has a negative impact on Mizo people and families. There are those who view Korean dramas as unimportant and useless. However, if we look closely, Korean dramas have many meanings and lessons beyond their appearance. The majority of Mizo people do not understand what they are trying to express.

Therefore, many of us do not appreciate Korean popular literature, we think it is meaningless and useless, and we do not try to understand the important things they express alongside their characters. One of the most obvious things that we don't see is the many characteristics of Mizo culture in Korean dramas.

Mizo culture is the way of life, family enviro

• • •

nment and lifestyle.So, how does Korean popular literature relate to Mizo culture? How South Korean dramas have portrayed Mizo culture is the main topic of this paper.

Rationale of the study

Indeed, K-dramas have played a crucial role in the global expansion of the Hallyu phenomenon. Starting in the 1990s, when the Korean culture began gaining traction worldwide, K-dramas have been steadily growing in popularity, earning millions of fans not just in Asia but across the entire globe. (Only you n.p)

Korean serials are mainly about family life, relationships and their lifestyle. Therefore, many people do not like it and do not appreciate it.And there are many people who think that it is just for women to watch and for women to enjoy.In Mizoram, when Korean serials became popular, many people criticized Korean serials for not containing the truth and media is also taking public opinion.

Many people think that it is just an expression of bad language learning and a bad family environment. Their views may seem right, but we see that their views are wrong. Angelo Lorenzo said , ' Literature is the foundation of humanity's cultures, beliefs, and traditions. It serves as a reflection of reality, a product of art, and a window to an ideology. Everything that happens within a society can be written, recorded in, and learned from a piece of literature.' H Laldinmawia said, 'Literature is related to life and Literature is defined as the mirror of life.' (Dinmawia) The truth of that is evident in these Korean serials.

It's time to throw away the criticism and contempt we have for trying to learn exactly the wrong things from Korean dramas. H. Laldinmawia said, 'Literature is about the joy of life, so it doesn't have to be about the good things of life.' (Dinmawia 11)We must also remember this.

There are many things we can learn from these Korean serials, the biggest of which is their culture. Their way of life, family management, social governance, clothing, food and treatment can be seen. That also taught me a lot of new things. Korean dramas portray Mizo's culture and Mizo's lifestyle. But we don't think about the Mizo culture and the good things they teach. The value of Korean popular literature is not understood by many of us because we focus only on the atmosphere of their language, Korean Serials that show Mizo culture and improvement are important for us to know.

What is Culture?

First, let us define what culture is. The Oxford Dictionary defined, 'The ideas, customs, and social behaviour of a particular people or society.' (Oxford dictionary np). Meriam Webster defined, 'The customary beliefs, social forms, and material traits of a racial, religious, or social groupalso : the characteristic features of everyday existence (such as diversions or a way of life) shared by people in a place or time.' (Merriam webster n.p)

According to E.B' Taylor, 'Culture... is that complex whole which includes knowledge, beliefs, arts, morals, law, customs, and any other capabilities and habits acquired by [a human] as a member of society." (Primitive culture 1 p 17) and Prof Darchhawna said, 'Culture is not only a personal characteristic and culture but also a national thing. It is not only born in the midst of changing times, but also a strong, growing and changing characteristic of a nation' (Thu leh hla May 2007 p 8).

What we see clearly from this, Culture is the way of life of a nation, the way of life of individuals, families, communities and the country as a whole. It is a thing that does not change in a short period of time and is embedded in the life of the nation.

Mizo Culture in Korean Popular Literature

Every nation has its own customs and traditions, handed down from ancestors and changed over time. Therefore, culture is a living thing. In South Korea, respect for the elderly is one of the most prominent cultures in Korea. It is also a place of authority and rule for men in their family and community management like Mizo society. In addition, spiritual beliefs, crafts, food and drink are popular in their culture and are preserved to this day.These cultures are very similar to Mizote culture.Let us examine the Mizo culture in Korean serials.

1. Daily life is dominated by male guidance within a primarily patriarchal society.

In Korea, men's rule and authority is highand the administration and management of the family, society and country is under the control of men.Boo Jin park also said in his research, 'Discussion of the power structure of the Korean family and the status of each member inevitably must begin with the traditional patriar-chal system.' (43)

Mahalat Saom Fudong described the origin of patriarchalism as follows, "Patriarchalism was reinforced in East Asian especially South Korea during the Choson period (1392-1910) which was brought through the beliefs derived from the teachings of Confucian and the patriarchal system flourished and developed in its own unique features along with the Confucian beliefs.' (122)

The 2009 hit Korean serial '3 Brothers' clearly depicts this culture. The father is a policeman and a good law enforcement officer. When there are important issues to be discussed in the family, he calls family meetings. When the father calls a meeting, they leave what they are doing and hold a meeting. They obeyed the father of the family and took his word seriously.

Kim Yi Sang and Joo Eo Young are in love. However, they did not agree to marry because their fathers had been enemies in the past. They were in love and wanted to get married, but their fathers told them not to marry. They took their father's word seriously and chose not to marry rather than suffer.This also shows that they respect their fathers and take their words seriously.

Boo Jin park said, 'As many aspects of everyday life were maintained through reciprocity with the agnatic kin in traditional Korean society, agnatic kin relations were emphasized.' (43) In a patriarchal society, men as well as their families are valued. In 3 Brothers serial, Kim Yi Sang and his wife did not celebrate the New Year at their women's house, and we see that Kim Yi Sang and wife went to the Kim Yi Sang house to celebrate the New Year.

Kim Hyun Chal's wife Do Woo-mi's words are also well known. 'Now that my father has allowed us to house, think about our house first. I'm going to find a new house.' This also shows that their father is the main holder of family power and decision-maker.And it was clearly stated in cruel temptation serial published in 2008.Jung Ha-jo is the head of the Jung family.The power of the family is in his hands, and he is the one who decides how to rule the family. He also owns a construction company and is the main breadwinner of his family. His wife Baek Mi-in was a card player, secretly playing cards with her friends without her husband's permission.Once, while playing cards, her husband came home and caught her. 'If you are still silent, take your clothes and leave my house immediately.' This also shows the authority and rule of the fathers in the household.

'Mizoculture is a patriarchal society, protecting their wife and children from enemies and beasts is considered as a man's duty and responsibility. Family and community management and discipline requires proper rules and regulations, which is the survival technique of Mizo as a nation.

In Mizo society, the king and his elders were in charge of the village administration, punishing those who committed crimes and violating the laws. Men are respected and valued as the hard workers of the household in the community. Patriarchal society has also become a prominent feature of South Korean culture.

2.The situation of women

The situation of women is very common theme in Korean serials. It is also a big part of Korean society and closely related to their culture.Wikipedia said, 'Gender inequality in South Korea is derived from deeply rooted patriarchal ideologies with specifically defined gender-roles.While gender inequality remains especially prevalent in South Korea's economy and politics, it has improved in healthcare and education.' This is probably true, as in Korea. In Mizo society, women status has also improved due to development. In Mizo society, women status has never been higher.

Women are to marry and live in other people's houses. Therefore, they did not even consider it necessary to study. After a marariage, woman follows the man's religion. Therefore, 'Women and crab have no religion' even the words came out. There was a saying in the old days, 'A wise woman does not cross the well. James Dokhuma said, 'This is because women are not considered to have authority beyond the well' (Dokhuma 287)

Women's status is not good. At home, they take care of all the household chores and they never had time to work in the fields during the day.They worked hard.Families without a man are especially pitiful.The position of women is still seen in Mizo culture and the South Korean drama/serial shows the situation of the woman.

Kamna Singh said, 'As Korean dramas play a vital, conscious and subconscious role in shaping the individual and society, such research is the need of the hour; more so as the global popularity of these dramas has made them the unofficial cultural ambassadors of Asia.' (1)He spoke about the importance of Korean dramas for society and culture. These societies and cultural shows also contain much to learn and study.

Wikepedia said, 'Confucian family values support traditional sex roles, with men expected to do "male-type" work and women expected to do "women-type" work. Since males are expected to be the major breadwinners in families, there is a strong cultural tendency to define females' roles as that of a wife, mother, and housekeeper.' In Mizo society, men are expected to do men's jobs, while women are expected to do "women's jobs."

The position of women in the family is portrayed in Korean serials, especially 3 Brothers and Cruel Temptation, because these two serials are family dramas.Research shows that, "In 1998, a Korean Women's Development Institute survey found that majority of South Korean women did all of the housework in their homes."

The status of women is still very much to be seen in Korean serials, and the status of women in the past has played a big role in their culture.3 Brothers serials also shows the position of women especially in the home. The character of Do Woo Mi is the biggest representation of the female position in 3 Brothers serial. Do Woo Mi (Kim Hee Jung) is the wife of Kim

Hyun Chal.

Kim Hyun Chal's brothers were unmarried for seven years. So for about 7 years he was in charge of all the household chores. She spends her days taking care of her husband and two sons, her parents and two brothers-in-law and he almost never had free time. She was very tired.There was no one else to help her, and she was a hardworking and righteous mother. A husband's family as well as her brothers and mothers were constantly harassing her. Sometimes they came to him for money, but it was a burden to him.

She gets up in the morning to cook and prepare her children's school meals. She was wearing an apron everytime and without even eating with his family. After cleaning the dining room and washing the dishes, he cooks for his mother in the afternoon. She has no time to do anything important. In the evening, when they don't eat together, there are many things to do.

For seven years, she took care of her husband and his family, but her husband and mother never repaid her with kindness.A husband's mother even criticized him for his mistake and she even rebuked them with harsh words.After seven years of hard work, her husband and mother were never good to her. Therefore she was very angry, and did not want to be silent as before. She was even sorry for himself.

In Episode 1, her husband buys her mother some fish. Do Woo Mi replied,'It's hard to tell your wife that I'm going to buy it for you.'She also said that he wanted to house. Her husband asked her who would take care of her parents. Here we see the position of the bride clearly, that her husband does not care about her and that he is only concerned about her mother. And we see that he doesn't appreciate his wife's hard work. We also see that the bride Doo Woo Mi wants to another house because she is so tired and she sees that her relationship with her husband is not getting better.

She was treated like a slave, and she had no time for himself. In the meantime, her husband's mother was criticizing her.She said to her husband, 'It is good that I have accepted her as your wife. We kept him safe.'According to the Domestic Violence Survey of South Korea in 2010, elder abuse was estimated to be 10%, physical abuse accounted for 2.2%, emotional abuse 9%, economic abuse 1.2%, and neglect 2.5%. Marital violence has been the most prevalent form of family violence in South Korea.

One of the predominant cause of domestic violence in the Republic of Korea is the presence of patriarchy in many domestic settings and patriarchal hegemony.The patrilineal house-head system (hojuje), which grants the succession rules to the paternal side of the family, was dominant in South Korea until the government abolished it in 2005.Research shows that the main reason for these violence and humiliation is the dominance of men in the family.

Mizo society has always considered widows to be inferior to ordinary women. In Korea, widows are also being looked down upon in their serials.In 3 Brother's, we see that they did not want a widow as their son's wife.

Their eldest son, Kim Geon Kang's wife, Uhm Chung Nan was secretly having children.When they know that she had a child and they were very angry. Do Woo Mi mother said, 'It's not a good thing to have a husband again. It's just very tiring every day.'The position of widows and the low status of women can be seen from these words. In this serial, Do Wo Mi is subjected to a lot of abuse and humiliation.

One day, she had a stomach ache and went to the hospital with difficulty, her husband called her and accused her of causing trouble. A husband's mother accused him of being sick and disobedient. And she also used his poverty and lack of education to insult her by comparing her to his eldest son's wife.Do Woo mi suffers from many illnesses not only physically but also mentally.

The author doesn't try to silence Do Woo Mi domestic abuse, but she also makes her express her rights. 'Mom, I have been married for over 10 years. I dedicated myself to my husband's family and did all the housework. I deserve to spend a little money when necessary.Besides, you are always looking for something to criticize me for.I'm not sure if I'm right or wrong, but I'm part of this family.'What is clear here is that the relationship between the husband's mother and the bride is the most common source of conflict.

It is also common in Mizo society. There are many people who want to move away. Most of these problems are caused by the mothers of their husbands, who are expected to work as servants and slaves.These husbands' mothers are the cause of many problems and difficulties.

Not only in 3 Brothers Serial, Cruel temptation also shows the position of women. Goo Yun Gee husband's mother, Baek Mi In, used her lack of education and family poverty to insult her. They could not have children. She worked hard but couldn't please her husband's mother. Even when he gave him the money, Baek Mi-in said, 'Is this all? Have you paid your family?' he accused her of stealing. A husband caught them playing cards. She even threw his hand at the bride.

Even after they leaders that their bride was dead, she was afraid of her soul. In Mizo Society, the husband's mother is the most vulnerable to the bride's wedding. We see that clearly. It is clearly shown that the cause of most of the suffering and pain of the bride, the conflict and difficulties between the bride and her husband is caused by the mother of the men.

3. Respect for the elderly

Respect for the elderly is an important part of Mizo society and Respect for the elderly is one of the most beautiful Mizo culture. That is the biggest and most proud Mizo culture. In the old days, they respected their elders and did not look down on them. Former Governor Major Mc. Call, ICS (1931-43) said, 'It is great that such a good and great life has been produced by such a nation, They were in the midst of a greater nation like China." The Chinese and Japanese are famous in the world for their respect for the elderly. Their culture is called 'Eastern Culture'. Mizo society in ancient times were not inferior to Chinese and Japanese in terms of their culture, respect for elders and friendship." (C Lalchawiliana np)

In ancient Mizo culture, respect for elders had a profound place. In Zawlbuk, children are led by their older brothers, if they need to be punished, they are punished. They respected the elders and never ate before the elders. In the countryside, the elders were not allowed to act. They pay attention to the elders' advice and follow the elders' advice in judgment. That large part of Mizo culture became one of the most prominent and prominent parts of South Korean culture. Commisceo Global said, 'Patriarchal obedience, cooperation, respect for elders, and familial piety are imbued into early childhood.'

They said that the importance of respect for elders and their teaching from childhood and that is the result. Kyu talk Sung and Han Sung Kim also said, 'Koreans, along with the Chinese and the Japanese, have practiced elder respect for generations. As Korea has undergone rapid industrialization, this age-old practice has become an issue of major concern for policy makers and gerontologists.' They also talked about respecting the elderly in Korean culture.

Respect for elders is the most common characteristic of Korean dramas. Every serial shows that Koreans respect their elders. This also shows that respect for the elderly is a part of their culture and everyone's heart. Reply 1988 is a Korean serial that shows Mizo society.

This serial is also very similar to Mizo life. Reply 1988 was published in 2015. Written by Lee Woo jung and directed by Shin Won Ho. Reply 1988 Genre is Family, Comedy and Romance. This serial is a portrayal of Mizo society. It is set in 1988 setting. The characters in the serial live in close relationships, even though they are teenagers, they respect their older brothers in every way. They consulted him in everything they did. That is a prominent feature of Mizo culture, and we see it in this serial. They went straight to their mother's mission without saying a word. Sung Deok Sun and his sister are often fighting, but he is afraid of his sister. He was so afraid and respectful that he ran home from school to put his shirt back. They were far away but he was afraid of his sister.

In 3 Brother's, Do Woo Mi said that, 'Uhm Chung Nan was talking too much to older people and didn't know how to behave.' Jeon Kwa Ja (Do Woo Mi husband's mother) also rebuked Do Woo Mi, 'Don't say anything you don't like when the older ones are talking.' These are the things that show their culture. The eldest wife greeted her husband's father separately. And the two protagonists, Kim Yi Sang and Joo Eo Young, want to get married. But both of their fathers refused.

The fact that they want to separate while in love because they want their father's happiness shows that they put the words of their eldest person ahead of them and respect their fathers. In Cruel Temptation and 3 Brothers, two bride are insulted by their husbands' mothers. We see that they are silent because they respect their elder person. In Korean dramas, respect for older people is felt when they meet each other. They bowed down to each other. They never passed each other without greeting each other. And Koreans are more respectful of their elders than Mizo's.

4. Religious rites and observances

Mizo elders are full of religious rites and observances. To be lawful and unlawful they have a lot. They also celebrate sacrifices to demons, offerings to the dead, and celebrations. Koreans also have their own festivals and religious rites. Comissceo Global said, 'Celebrations for these festivals are based around ancestors, family, games, harvest festivals and food.'

Encyclopedia of Korean Folk Culture, 'Gijesa is a term referring to a Confucian memorial rite held to honor the ancestors at the earliest hour on the anniversary of their death with food offerings prepared the day before. Koreans have maintained this tradition to remember and honor their ancestors on this day. Mizo's have also prepared food for the dead since ancient times. They believe that the spirits of their dead relatives do not go to the grave but remain in the house and its surroundings. Therefore, when they eat, they prepare a meal and invite them to eat. From the story of Tlingi and Ngama, we learn that there was no good food and drink in the village of the dead, so Ngama put their fresh vegetables in the grave for Tlingi. From here, the preparation of vegetables for the dead was prepared. It is an important part of South Korean culture we see it in their dramas.

In the Dong Yi serial, the protagonist Dong Yi's father and uncle are killed by soldiers for conspiracy. On the anniversary of their death, Dong Yi went to the mountain where they died and prepared this Gijesa for them. He spent his time carrying vegetables for food and drink. And we see that his brother also spent this time.

The Soul of Seol said, 'The first thing to do is prepare the various food dishes. This can be done the week prior to the event. Various meats, fruits, and vegetable dishes should be prepared.' Thus, the preparation method is described.

Alcohol has a profound place in South Korean culture and Mizo culture.They are also used in religious rites and ceremonies. In Korea, as we have seen in many serials, alcohol is used by friends and family on their sad or happy days. At the same time, there are almost no drunks. In ancient Mizo society, alcohol was used on festive occasions, happy and sad days. However, there were never any drunkenness.

Their teaching is also very good. Even in Korean serials about alcohol, we see the meaning of appreciating Korean culture. At the same time, we can see the similarities with Mizo culture. Doo Wo mi was unhappy and drank alcohol. Her husband said, 'You smell alcohol in the afternoon. My mother will know and she will be angry with you. ' From what he said, we see that women's drinking is not beautiful and that it is not beautiful to smell alcohol in the presence of older men.

And Joo Eo Young rebuked his sister, 'What would you do if you drank late into the night and got into trouble. You"ll be drunk in the street. You'll embarrass my father, what can you do?' From this we see that they do not want to drink alcohol at all and that they consider drunkenness to be a shame and a disgrace. It is also very similar to the Mizo's views and guidelines.

5. Volunteerism and neighborliness

Volunteering is the most prominent part of Mizo culture. Since ancient times, volunteers and hardworking people have been the most respected people in the community. James Dokhuma said, 'Mizo society is made happy by unselfishness. Unselfishness has a widespread place in Mizo society. The king secretly looked at the unselfishness men. Those who deserve to be honored are respected in the kingdom. That is an exciting thing. (Dokhuma 242-243)

In Mizo society, young men are the guardians of the village and the people. The brave and volunteer young men were honored by the king with wine and gifts and they also play an important role in society. They are very competitive in volunteering, and without these rewards, volunteering would have been a bet in their lives.

In the Dong Yi serial, the character's Dong Yi, is a volunteer and brave woman who loves justice.She hated injustice, he dared to investigate alone and face the enemy, and he feared no one in his righteousness. She stood up for righteousness at the risk of his life, and never feared his enemies. And she takes action even after others are not ready or disappointed. Dong Yi's character is a characteristic of Mizo heroes. In this character, we see the volunteerism, courage, and even the life of sacrifice for friends. Even when the queen was expelled, she was determined to find out her rights. Even when his friends told him not to go, she said, 'But I don't want to let this opportunity pass. This is a good opportunity to show the queen's righteousness." We see that she tried to go to a dangerous place.

The serial shows the courage and bravery of Mizo life. Mizo's are very friendly to their neighbours, and they are very supportive of each other in good times and bad times. They lived together as a family, shared their needs, shared food and drinks, and had a good relationship. They knew the value of neighbors, so they said, 'It is better to fight seven cities than to fight a neighbor.'

Korean culture is also a neighborly culture. In Reply 1988, we saw a lot of neighborly love. In today's developing and busy world. However, we don't even care about our neighbors. We don't even know the value of neighbors. We don't even pay attention to the value of neighbors and the love of neighbors. Reply 1988 is also clearly stated for this purpose.

In Reply 1988, the friends are watching tv at a friend's house. When it was time to eat, the mothers called out to their children. These are very similar to Mizo life, children playing until dark in the evening and being called by their mothers and fathers when they are about to eat. They are willing to share their possessions and things they don't have. This also clearly reflects Mizo culture.

Conclusion :

There are many things that are clear from the above. Korean Drama is very important and there are many things to learn. For Mizos themselves, respect for elders, volunteerism and dedication, neighborly love, the position of men in the family and the way we view women have given us many lessons to learn. There are many similarities between Korean culture and Mizo culture. There are many beliefs that Mizote are from the northwest.

Mizo and Korean people are similar in appearance, language and food. Therefor, Korean films and serials are easy to relate to and enjoyable for Mizo. Korean dramas teach viewers the importance of respecting the elderly and the importance of maintaining respect for the elderly. It also shows us the causes of women's suffering and the causes of domestic problems. The characters are very similar to Mizo. Korean serials are characterized by angry conversations. In ancient Mizo life, couples did not speak politely in their homes. That's why it's not just these fights and harsh word, their stories and teachings are very important.

They preserve and promote their culture through their dramas and films. Also Mizo's culture should be preserved and promoted through these films and serials. These things we have learned show that Korean serials have a lot of content and research. It is an important knowledge of their culture and society, and at the same time it is a source of information about Mizo culture.

• • •

• • •

Work Cited

1. Commiscio Global. Com. https://www.commisceo-global.com/resources/country-guides/south-korea-guide.
2. Dinmawia, H. Literature Lamtluang. K. L Offset Printers. 2020
3. Dokhuma, James. Hmanlai Mizo Kalphung. R. Lalrawna. 2015
4. Fudong, Mahalat Saom. Patriarchal Society Of Kore. A Case Study On Korean Comfort Women. International Journal of Advance Research in Science and Engineering. Volume No.07 Issue No 04, April 2018

Soft yet Manly: Redefining Masculinity in Korean & Chinese Dramas and its acceptance among Indian Female Spectators

Dr. Amita, Assistant Professor, Department of Journalism & Mass Communication, Banaras Hindu University, Varanasi, UP, India

Aditi Khare, Ph.D. Research Scholar, Department of Journalism & Mass Communication, Banaras Hindu University, Varanasi, UP, India

Abstract

The representation of male characters in the contemporary Korean-Chinese dramas are trying to break the chain of hegemonic masculinity which has become toxic for society. This research used qualitative content analysis to analyze the representation of masculinity and compare them with the existing notions of masculinity. The researchers also investigated the acceptance of redefined masculinity in Korean and Chinese dramas by Indian female spectators through a data of 40 respondents collected through questionnaires.

Imagining a man being sensitive, emotional, doing household chores, less dominating, and gentle is a bit tough because these traits are identified as feminine in most of the parts of the world. This is why most of the Indian directors-script writers are still representing the hegemonic masculine traits in their films and series. But the Korean and Chinese dramas are challenging the existing notions of masculinity and redefining it and the Indian audience especially female spectators are watching them. Data from UK-based YouGov's report of 2019 says that 55% of Indians now watch foreign language content. Netflix data in 2020 reported that viewershipofKorean dramas increased by 370 percent from 2019 in India.

This study found that there is actually a balanced representation of both soft and hegemonic masculine traits and the toxic masculinity is not depicted in the dramas. It also reveals that more than a half of total respondents appreciate and accept the redefined masculine traits portrayed in the Korean and Chinese Dramas.

Keywords: Korean Dramas, Chinese Dramas,Representation, Hegemonic masculinity, Softmasculinity, Indian female spectators

Introduction

A defined by the Council of Europe, "Masculinities are those behaviors, languages, and practices, existing in specific cultural and organizational locations, which are commonly associated with men, thus culturally defined as not feminine." One needs to fit within the socially constructed traits to be recognized as a male. Although the understanding of masculinity is not the same everywhere, it differs across time and socio-cultural contexts, and within groups as well based on varying characteristics.. The word masculine is derived from the Latin word *masculinus* which means having the exact qualities of the male gender that are constructed with time by society and its culture. Whereas the word feminine is derived from Latin word *femininus* means the feminine has traits like gentleness, delicacy, prettiness, and so on.Feminist writer, Simone de Beauvoir puts it *'One is not born a man but becomes one, 'one is not born a woman but becomes one.'* This statement explains that masculine and feminine traits are socially constructed and the males and the females are expected to behave within these constructions. The Washington Post in their article mentioned that it is not easy to define what actually masculine is but the stereotypical notion goes like this: A "real man" is someone who is physically strong, a protector, stoic and unemotional. He doesn't display his weakness or ask for help or be vulnerable in front of his friends, family, or colleagues. In simpler terms masculinity which is legitimized with time and is currently termed hegemonic masculinity is closely associated with the word muscle, which indicates physical power or strength (Azizah & Dwiyanti, 2021)

These set behaviors about masculinity like being aggressive, muscular, dominant, protective, responsible, and so on are almost similar in various other countries as well (Azizah & Dwiyanti, 2021). A study on the intersection of masculinity and health by Dr. Wizdom Powell (associate professor of psychiatry at Uconn Health) says that, "The common narrative that teaches men and boys to not cry, take things like a man under any circumstances leads to the habitual practice of not expressing anyone about their pain or worries which could have significant implications. There are downstream consequences when there is no healthy outlet to dispense negative emotions. These bottled-up negative emotions pop up behaviorally in another way like being aggressive, controlling, dominating, abusing, and so on."

This is why there is a growing movement to reform certain notions and reject society's rigid definition of masculinity and redefine what it means to be a man. So, the counter to the hegemonic masculinity is termed as soft masculinity which talks about a new man or metrosexual man who treats people in a more subtle and gentler way (Miyose & Engstrom). They are emotionally understanding and believe in the concept that even men being muscular and strong can be pretty, beautiful and fashionable.

Korea started to represent soft masculinity in their dramas, band performances, advertisements and so on, to counter the hegemonic masculinity. This actually worked for them as their content started to spread in the western countries and was praised by the citizens and nowadays even it is accepted in Asian countries as well (Ainslie, 2017). According to UK-based YouGov's report of 2019, 55% of Indians now watch foreign language content. In India, the viewership for Korean dramas increased by 370 percent from 2019 (Netflix, 2020). Not only Websites but TV channels have also started to stream these shows in India. The technology of subtitling and Hindi dubbing are playing a great role in the growth of viewership.

Earlier, even Korean dramas portrayed hegemonic masculinity as per its culture within four major norms: Power, Opposition toward femininity, Domination and objectification of nature, and the Avoidance of emotion (Miyose & Engstrom). Also, Chinese dramas based on their culture of Confucian masculinity represented hegemonic masculinity. But contemporary Korean and Chinese director-scriptwriter are portraying the soft masculine traits in their dramas. Koreans were the first one to initiate this change in representation and that's why Chinese dramas are still behind them in the competition. Maliangkay (2013/2014) in his studies mentioned how Koreans have changed their roles in the way they advertise their products. They have started the commodification of males in their beauty products ads to cater to the female gaze and it is working there.

Moreover, these dramas are having a huge viewership in India and this paper focuses on analyzing the masculine traits that Korean and Chinese Dramas represent on screen and how are they in contrast with the hegemonic masculinity that prevails in Asia. Also, it focuses on finding out the reasons behind the increased viewership of these dramas, especially among the Indian Female audiences.

Review of Literature

Azizah & Dwiyanti (2021), in their studies, titled *South Korea un reconstructing masculinity as brand image of the state's economic diplomacy* have applied the theory of Economic Diplomacy, Public

Diplomacy, and State Identity to analyze the reasons behind the promotion of soft masculinity through K-Pop and Korean Dramas. By applying the phenomenology method and qualitative research method, they have studied the South Korean Government and found that the K-Pop and K-Dramas help in attracting global audience to Korea. This study also revealed that South Korea is utilizing soft masculinity as its brand image to improve economic diplomacy for its cosmetic industry.

Amaran & Wen (2018), research work focused to find out the *Factors of watching Korean dramas among youth in Kuching city, Malaysia.* They used quantitative data analysis, descriptive analysis, and factor analysis methods to analyze the data of 300 respondents collected through questionnaires. The study revealed that Learning and Sociability were the two factors among youth of Kuching City to watch Korean Dramas and the factors were studied using the uses and gratification theory.

Ainslie (2017), astudy titled *Korean Soft Masculinity vs. Malay Hegemony: Malaysian masculinity and Hallyu Fandom* examines the feedback provided by a number of Malaysian male fans of Korean popular culture. The analysis found that such fandom does not necessarily provides the basis for a complete rejection of patriarchy, it just gives a critique to the pre-existing notions. It also explained that such content helps in constructing accessible and alternative form of masculine identity in contrast to hegemonic masculinity.

Khai & Wahab (2017), in their study titled *Prettiness as a shield: The romantic Perpetuation of Patriarchy through the representation of Pretty Boy in Popular Korean Dramas in Malaysia* studied the representation of metrosexual characters in the selected dramas using qualitative content analysis. This study found that the concept of metro sexuality is redefined in Korean dramas as the "pretty boy" both technically and visually, their features like slim face, silky hair, and fair skin, and the male characters also exhibit both feminine and masculine traits in the term pretty boy. Although, the researcher observed that in the outside world the social position of man is higher than women and the feminized form of man is limited to his appearance and emotions that too only in private space, this signifies that the patriarchal framework is deeply rooted in governing gender differences.

Miyose & Engstrom (2015), in their work titled *Boys Over Flowers and the Making of the "New Man"* investigated hegemonic masculinity and counterhegemonic masculinity depicted in the K- drama Boys Over Flowers through textual analysis. The study found that the content showed the transformation from hegemonic to new/ soft masculinity. The show also portrayed violence in a repurposed form and a female in a more empowered and logical form.

The rationale of the study

As per the reports of Netflix, the viewership of Korean dramas in India has increased by more than 370 percent in 2020 from 2019 (Economic Times, 2021). Few other reports have also shown an increase in demand for Korean and Chinese Dramas. This growth of the Korean wave and the initiation of demand for Chinese TV series among Indian audience points toward the study of Korean and Chinese Dramas content. Among several factors in Korean and Chinese Dramas, this study particularly analyzes the representation of soft masculinity and compare it with the hegemonic model of masculinity. This research also focuses on understanding why Indian females are watching these dramas.

Research Objectives

1. To analyze the representation of redefined masculinity in contemporary Korean and Chinese Dramas.
2. To compare the represented masculinity with the hegemonic masculinity.
3. To investigate the acceptance of redefined masculinity in Korean and Chinese dramas among Indian female spectators.

Research Questions

1. How is masculinity redefined in contemporary Korean and Chinese Dramas and to what extent?
2. Do the Indian female audiences actually accept and appreciate the masculinity represented in the Korean and Chinese Dramas?
3. What are the reasons for acceptance and appreciation of redefined masculinity in Korean and Chinese dramas among Indian female spectators?

Research Methodology

This research is based on both qualitative and quantitative studies. The researchers have used qualitative content analysis to analyze the representation of redefined masculinity in selected Korean and Chinese Dramas. Based on purposive sampling, two Korean dramas and two Chinese

Dramas with the highest ratings were selected based on the ratings provided by websites like IMDb, Netflix, and My Drama List. On the other hand, to understand whether Indian females accept the redefined masculinity in these dramas or not,researchers have collected data through a questionnaire through Google form.The targeted sample of Indian female audience is selected onthe basis of stratified sampling. As the research focuses only on those Indian females who have ever watched Korean or Chinese dramas to obtain more accurate results. The sample size of this study is 50 respondents as per the availability of required respondents in the restricted time. The questionnaires werecirculatedto the respondents through an online survey link using the snowball technique to collect the data. In order to minimize bias as much as possible, the random sampling method was also used to enable respondents with different education levels, age groups, ethnicity, and relationship status to have an equal chance to be selected.

Representation of redefined masculinity in Korean and Chinese Dramas: A qualitative content analysis

The researchers chose two contemporary Korean dramas; *Crash Landing on You (2019, Rom-com)* and *It's Okay not to be Okay (2020, Rom-Com)* based on the highest ratings provided by IMDb, Netflix, and My Drama list. Similarly, two Chinese dramas; *Who Rules the World (2022, Action and Romance)* and *Love O2O (2016, Rom-Com and Gaming)* were selected based on the highest ratings provided by Rakuten Viki, IMDb, and My Drama List.

To analyze the representation of masculinity in the selected dramas, the content analysis method isused in the study. The researchers created an MS Excel sheet to note down the redefined masculine traits (Soft masculine traits) represented in each episode of these dramas. Also, the hegemonic masculine traits were also noted to compare the transformation in the represented masculine traits. A comparison chart taken from previous research was used to specify the hegemonic masculine and soft masculine traits to compare and observe the transformation between the two.

Comparison between hegemonic masculinity vs. soft masculinity
Physical traits of Hegemonic Masculinity

1. Muscular, buffed body
2. Tanned skin
3. Defined facial feature
4. Thick facial and body hair

Mental traits of Hegemonic Masculinity

- Lack of emotion
- Dominant
- Aggressive
- Focus and physical strength

Physical traits ofSoft Masculinity

1. Lean, sculpted body
2. Fair skin
3. Soft facial feature
4. Lack of facial and body hair

Mental traits of Soft Masculinity

1. More emotional
2. Less dominant
3. Gentle
4. Focus on intelligence and mental strength

In the Korean Drama, *Crash Landing on You,* the male lead Ri Jeong Hyeok is in the armed forces of North Korea and encounters a girl from South Korea who accidentally lands in his nation. Another Korean drama, *Twenty-FiveTwenty-One* portrayed the male lead with similar traits. In this drama, the male lead, Yi Jin is a financially struggling college student. He is into several part-time jobs which portrays that he is dependent on himself for his living as he didn't want to be a burden on his bankrupt parents. Their characters portrayed both hegemonic and soft masculine traits. The masculinity represented in these dramas tried to create a balance between hegemonic and soft masculine traits. The characters were protective, respectful, and calm not only towards females but also towards males. But the domination and aggressive side were also shown whenever required, which was need of the hour. Yet in several scenes, the character seemed to be dominated by the female leads and the male leads don't even get offended when females yell at them. Soft masculine traits like cooking, being shy, soft-hearted and gentle, using mental strength, showing concern, crying, and lack of facial hair and body hair were prominently represented in the drama. On the other hand, hegemonic masculine traits like being protective seem to be overly done in some situations. Whereas other traits like domination and aggressiveness were not shown as being too much they were incorporated as per the requirement of the situation.

In the Chinese Drama, *Who Rules the World*, the male lead Feng Lan Xi is the son of an emperor. In the initial episodes, he disguises himself as a physically weak person and mentally very sharp in front of everyone except a few. In the later episodes, he exposes himself as a strong martial art fighter and also an intelligent thinker. In this drama, the female lead is also from a royal family and also a martial art fighter. This drama is set in an ancient period, yet the representation of masculinity is not toxic. The male is very much supportive and appreciates the female lead. He is not offended by the fact that she is equal to him in the martial art world, she also becomes the queen of her father's kingdom.

In the other drama, *Love O2o*, the male lead Xiao Nai, is an engineering student who plays games and is also a game developer. Here also, the female lead is an equally skilled game player and this does not offend the male lead which is a positive trait. He is overly protective but also gives his girl space to be with her space.

In both, the dramas, soft masculine traits like cooking, being shy, logical, using the brain more than physical strength, and having no facial hair are shown prominently in all the episodes. Other traits like domination, aggressiveness, and controlling are shown as and when needed and not overly done.

Acceptance of redefined masculinity in Korean and Chinese dramas among Indian female spectators: A quantitative analysis

The researcher created a mixed Questionnaire for this research, which has both open and close-ended questions. Questionnaires were shared through an online survey link using the snowball technique targeting 50 respondents but only 40 responses were received within the time limit. So, the data analysis is based on the 40 responses. The graphical representation and response table of all questions is given below-

Discussion and Conclusion

The content analysis of this study found that the contemporary Korean and Chinese dramas are making a good attempt in creating a balance in representing both usual masculine traits which we call hegemonic and the soft masculine traits. The soft masculine traits like being understanding, emotionally expressive, less dominating, using more of mental strength and avoiding unnecessary use of physical strength and aggressive behavior. The masculinity represented in these dramas is less toxic as compared to what was portrayed and shown in series of earlier times. This is a good step that can bring a transformation in the masculinity and make it less toxic for men, women and for the society as well.

The data collected from the Indian female audience revealed that more than a half of total respondents actually appreciate and accept the redefined masculinity which is represented in the contemporary Korean and Chinese dramas. The data showed that majorly the age group of 15-30 , students and single women are indulged in these dramas. 62.5 % of the respondents prefer Korean dramas, 22.5% prefer both Korean and Chinese while only 7.5% prefer Chinese dramas, it will take time for Chinese dramas to earn more Indian female audience. The most preferred genre of the respondents was Romance, Rom-Com, Fantasy and few also enjoy Action and Thriller dramas . Out of the mentioned factors in the questionnaire, the data showed that the spectators watch these dramas majorly for entertainment, relaxation, learning (culture and language), and escapism. They are hooked to these dramas because of the great storylines, and the male-female characterization. One question asked if they like the man performing household chores the data showed that 90% of respondents are in favor and also wants Indian man to participate in it as it can share the load of women and this will bring gender equality which is required in this era The Indian female who watches these dramas also expressed that they also relate to the female leads of these dramas sometimes . The most appealing traits for the respondents among the represented masculine traits were the way they care, love and understand their partners and families, their looks, dressing and appearance, and the way they portray their emotions, and also their financial status or the way they struggle for their career. The responses reflect that the female like the man who are more considerate, tender, gentle and understanding but few of them also like their dominant and controlling behavior. They like men with both angry young man behavior and soft masculine traits basically a balance of both where they also get the space. The masculine traits that the respondent shared in the open-ended question which they do not like in these Korean and Chinese dramas were the portrayal of rich and influential male story, they are over protective, sometimes they hide their emotions. Whereas, few respondents wrote that they like the protective behavior. So, it can be interpreted as the it depends on females what they prefer but the majority doesn't like the over protective masculine traits which is shown in these dramas.

This research paper revealed that the directors and script writers of Korea and China are actually making a good attempt in redefining the representation of masculine traits in Korean and Chinese dramas. They have portrayed the soft-masculine traits prominently without loosing the essence of masculinity. The data also found that the majority of Indian female audience who watches these dramas are actually appreciating and accepting those soft masculine traits. This transformation in the representation of masculinity tells that the hegemonic masculinity needs to be changed for the betterment of both men and women and the society as well. To cater the socially constructed standards to be identified as a man, men go through a lot and research studies have revealed that the extreme dominant, aggressive and controlling behavior most of the times results after the bottled-up negative emotions.

This study only focused on identifying that whether the masculine traits are hegemonic orcounterhegemonic, future studies can conduct an in-depth analysis of the dialogues and gestures to study it in more detail. This research only studied the Indian female audiences that too on a small sample, so, future work can be done on a larger sample for more accurate results.

References

1. Elfving-Hwang, Joanna. (2017). "Aestheticizing Authenticity: Corporate Masculinities in Contemporary South Korean Television Dramas." Asia Pacific Perspectives, Vol. 15, no. 1, 55-72.
2. Miyose, Colby & Engstrom, Erika. (2015). Boys Over Flowers: Korean Soap Opera and the Blossoming of a New Masculinity. Popular Culture Review. 26. 2-13. 10.18278/pcr.26.2.1.
3. Maliangkay, Roald. (2013/2014). "Catering to the Female Gaze: The Semiotics of Masculinity in Korean Advertising." Australian National University. Pg, 43-61.
4. Liu, F. (2019). Chinese Young Men's Construction of Exemplary Masculinity: The Hegemony of Chenggong. Men and Masculinities, 22(2), 294–316. https://doi.org/10.1177/1097184X17696911
5. Wen, H. (2014). "Diversifying" masculinity: super girls, happy boys, cross-dressers, and real men on Chinese media. *ASIANetwork Exchange: A Journal for Asian Studies in the Liberal Arts*, 21(1), pp.16–26. DOI: http://doi.org/10.16995/ane.75

6. Amaran, Mazdan & Wen, Lau. (2018). Factors of watching Korean Drama Among Youth in Kuching City, Malaysia. International Journal of Arts and Commerce. Vol. 7, No.7, 33-48.

7. Ainslie, Mary. (2017). Korean soft masculinity vs. Malay hegemony: Malaysian masculinity and Hallyu fandom. Korea Observer. Institute of Korean Studies. Vol. 48, No. 3, pp. 609-638.

8. William Jankowiak & Xuan Li (2014) The Decline of the Chauvinistic Model of Chinese Masculinity: A Research Report, Chinese Sociological Review, 46:4, 3-18, DOI: 10.2753/CSA2162-0555460401.

9. Soh, Weng Khai & Wahab, Juliana. (2017). Prettiness as a Shield: The Romantic Perpetuation of Patriarchy through the Representation of Pretty Boy in Popular Korean Dramas in Malaysia. Media Watch. 8. 298-310. 10.15655/mw/2017/v8i3/49153.

10. Song, Geng. (2010). Chinese Masculinities Revisited: Male Images in Contemporary Television Drama Serials. Modern China. 36(4), 404-434.

11. The Economic Times. (2021). The 'K' magic is taking over India: People find comfort in Korean dramas, music, and food. https://economictimes.indiatimes.com/magazines/panache/the-k-magic-is-taking-over-india-people-find-comfort-in-korean-dramas-music-and-food/articleshow/86836620.cms?from=mdr

12. Pal, Deepanjana. (2021). Why Indians are fascinated by K-dramas. India Today. New Delhi. https://www.indiatoday.in/magazine/leisure/story/20210510-why-indians-are-fascinated-by-k-dramas-1797047-2021-05-01

13. IANS. (2021). India's romance with Korean dramas gives way to K-craze among desi fans. Entertainment Times. Times of India. https://timesofindia.indiatimes.com/web-series/news/korean/indias-romance-with-korean-dramas-gives-way-to-k-craze-among-desi-fans/articleshow/83504994.cms

A study of Translation Strategies used in the Hindi Dubbing of Top Gun: Maverick and Minions: The Rise of Gru

Aswin Kumar DBVN, PhD Scholar, CALTS, University of Hyderabad, Hyderabad - 46
Naresh Annem, Assistant Professor, CALTS, University of Hyderabad, Hyderabad - 46

Abstract

Audiovisual media is reliant on multiple channels of communication for meaning-making. Dubbing is one of the audiovisual translation modalities that focuses on verbal utterances. Transferring meaning by replacing the original voice track with that of the target language, dubbing is a tool to make a film available to global viewers across cultures. In India, from dubbing children's entertainment shows to the dubbing of large-scale commercial films, this translation modality has seen unprecedented growth in the entertainment space in the past two decades. The current study aims to explicate the translation strategies used in the Hindi dubbing of *Top Gun: Maverick* (2022), an American action-thriller, and *Minions: The Rise of Gru* (2022), a computer-animated children's film. The disparities between films intended for adult viewers and those geared towards children are the determinants in the choice of these films. The concepts of Foreignization and Domestication and translation strategies proposed by Irene Ranzato are used as theoretical background for this study. Using comparative analysis and focusing on the translation of culture specific references, this study attempts to determine the most commonly used translation strategies and highlights the differences in the dubbing of the aforementioned films.

*Keywords:*Dubbing, Audiovisual Translation, Translating Culture, CulturalSpecificity, Translation Strategy

Introduction

Audiovisual content uses two components - sound and images for the representation of meaning. Audiovisual translation is a strand of translation that involves the transference of verbal elements in audiovisual materials from one language to another (Chiaro, 2012). The integration of sound and visual components adds a layer of complexity to the translation process compared to the translation of the written text. Developments in communication technology and the resultant increase in the circulation of audiovisual materials and the growing inter-dependence between audiovisual translation and technological innovation are the two developments that have caused a sharp increase in interest in audiovisual translation (Pérez-González, 2014). Dubbing, subtitling, and voiceover are considered the most prominent modes of audiovisual translation (Díaz Cintas, 2009). Dubbing involves transferring meaning from one language to another by replacing the original voice track with that of the target language. Subtitling entails written text on the screen that presents the verbal language and other sounds used in the audiovisual content in a written form. Voiceover is the superimposition of a target language voice track over the original voice track. In the case of voiceover, the original audio track is at a reduced volume.

Audiovisual translation has advanced in different ways in different countries. While both dubbing and subtitling are flourishing businesses across the world, countries favour one mode over the other. One of the primary considerations in the choice of translation mode is the cost of labour and technology involved in the process. Dubbing is more expensive than subtitling, so much so it is cost prohibitive in some cases. European countries, like France, Germany, and Italy, favour dubbing over subtitling, while countries with smaller film industries, such as Belgium, Netherlands, and Switzerland, tend to favour subtitling (Pérez-González, 2014). A survey conducted by YouGov in 2019 concluded that among Indian audiences watching audiovisual content, 72% of the sampling preferred subtitles, while 24% preferred watching the dubbed versions (Sharma, 2019).

Translators encounter various constraints in the process of audiovisual translation. Professional, formal, linguistic, semiotic or iconic, and sociocultural constraints hinder translation (Chaume, 2020). Culture specific references are entities that belong distinctively to a culture, and they can be visual, verbal or both visual and verbal in nature (Chiaro, 2009). These items can be mapped into geographical references, ethnographic references, and socio-political references (Díaz Cintas &Remael, 2007). In addition to the challenges apposite to audiovisual translation, translators of dubbing and subtitles are confronted with issues in translating references pertaining to a specific culture, language specific references and references that are related to both culture and language (Chiaro, 2009). Translating culture specific references from one language to another pose a challenge to the translator due to the possible unavailability of appropriate equivalents in the target culture. Translators use various strategies like loaning, calque, replacing the source culture specific item with a target culture specific item etc. in translating culture specific references.

Top Gun: Maverick, released in 2022, is an American film directed by Joseph Kosinski. The protagonist, played by Tom Cruise, is the navy's top aviator and is tasked with a special assignment which tests not only his skill as an aviator but also his mental strength in dealing with his past. This film is an action drama geared toward an adult audience. *Minions: The Rise of Gru*, released in 2022, is an American film directed by Kyle Balda. The story revolves around a boy named Gru who aspires to be a supervillain, a troop of yellow henchmen called the minions and a group of supervillains named Vicious 6. The story is set in the 1970s, as the film's initial scene indicates, and is an action-comedy film geared towards children.

Rationale of the study and Research questions

Audiovisual translation has been a comparatively unknown domain of research until the end of the previous century but has seen a substantial increase in interest in the past two decades (Díaz Cintas, 2009). Some areas of audiovisual translation, like dubbing and subtitling, have provided large spaces for research. Advances in communication technology and the ease of access to online resources resulted in the burgeoning audiovisual content that is shared across countries. This necessitates research of areas like the translation of culture within the ambit of audiovisual translation. Focussing on dubbing culture specific references, the current research attempts to answer the below research questions:

1. Which dubbing strategy is most frequent in translating culture specific references to Hindi in the films *Top Gun: Maverick* and *Minions: The Rise of Gru*?
2. Does the difference in the target audience for the films *Top Gun: Maverick* and *Minions: The Rise of Gru* contribute to the selection of a specific dubbing strategy over other strategies when translating culture specific references?

Section 1 of this research paper gives a brief introduction to audiovisual translation and defines the key terms used in this study. In section 2, the rationale of the study is presented, and research questions are defined.

Section 3 describes the theoretical framework, and research methodology is described in section 4. Section 5 discusses the findings of the research before making concluding comments in section 6

Theoretical Framework

Adapting the taxonomy proposed by Díaz Cintas and Remael (2007) for translation strategies employed in subtitling, Irene Ranzato put forth eleven dubbing strategies that were used in her study that focused on three television series that were dubbed into Italian. Ranzato (2016) proposed the following eleven strategies for dubbing:

i.   Loan: translation by a literal repetition of the culture specific reference from the source text to the target text.

ii. Official translation: translation that uses a well-established equivalent in the target culture.

iii. Calque: represents a literal translation of the culture specific reference.

iv. Explication: translation by addition of information that is not present in the source culture specific reference. This strategy is not always feasible due to the limitation on the number of words a translator can add to the text.

v.   Generalisation by hypernym: translation by replacing the source culture specific reference with a hypernym that gives a broader meaning.

vi. Concretisation by hyponym: translation by replacing the source culture specific reference with a hyponym that gives a specific meaning instead of a broader one.

vii. Substitution: translation by substituting a concept closer to the source culture with another one that is closer to the target culture.

viii. Lexical recreation: translation by coining new words/phrases in the target language.

ix. Compensation: situation where loss at one point in translation is compensated by addition/gain at another point

x.   Elimination: situation when a source culture specific reference is not translated into the dubbed version.

xi. Creative addition: Addition by intervention of the adapter to add words/ phrases closer to the target culture (Ranzato, 2016).

Research Methodology

The current study is a qualitative study based on contrastive analysis of films. Comparative film analysis is the method used for the current research, with a focus on the dubbing of culture specific references. The original movies in English were watched, and culture specific references were identified by following the definition from section 1. The dubbed versions in Hindi were then watched to document how the identified culture specific references are translated to Hindi in the process of dubbing. This list was then classified according to the translation strategies described in section 3 to identify the most frequently used translation strategy.

Data Analysis

Culture specific references that are considered impolite in the source culture have been substituted with acceptable target culture references. For example, "Knock it off" (Kosinski, 2022, 41:31) is dubbed as "Drill Khatam". The expression "Knock it off", which is considered impolite in the source culture, is replaced in the dubbed version by an utterance that suits the context (completion of the drill) instead of an impolite expression. Similarly, "Loser!" (Balda, 2022, 08:19) is replaced by "super villain banega!", in a sarcastic tone in the Hindi version. Expletives and other obscene words are substituted with target culture acceptable words/ phrases. In comparison, there are no instances of expletives in *Minions: The Rise of Gru* owing to it being a children's film; 11 out of 12 obscene words/ phrases in *Top Gun: Maverick* were replaced by target culture acceptable words/phrases. For example, "Holy s**t" (Kosinski, 2022, 12:08, 01:22:19) has been dubbed to "Areynahin" and "Wah maza" respectively.

In most cases, substitution was used as a translation strategy by transposition, where "cultural concept of one culture is replaced by a cultural concept from another" (Díaz Cintas and Remael, 2007, p. 204). An example of this is "As I live and breathe" (Kosinski, 2022, 44:44), which is dubbed as "Aapaayebahaaraayi". The phrase "As I live and breathe", in the source culture, is used to stress the truth of a statement. However, as this does not hold the same currency in the target culture, it is replaced by a phrase closer to the target culture. Similarly, "You give 'em hell" (Kosinski, 2022, 01:28:06) is dubbed as "Unki band baja do" and "They better start pulling their weight around here" (Balda, 2022, 12:33) is dubbed as "gharmeinmuft ki rotiyaannathodekuchkaambhikarein". A similar dubbing strategy is used to substitute proper names that are rooted in the source culture. For example, "Easy there Don Rickles...who is Don Rickles?" (Balda, 2022, 54:03) is dubbed as "Jabaansambhal half ticket...half ticket kaunhai?".

Substitution thru generalisation by hypernym is observed in "Nine-ball, Bob...rack 'em" (Kosinski, 2022, 26:06) dubbed as "Billiards,

Bob...kheloge?". Nine-ball and rack are words specific to a sport that many Indians are not familiar with. Substituting Nine-ball with the hypernym Billiards makes it more understandable to an Indian audience.

Elimination is another strategy that has been used. For example, "it's a dog fight all the way home" (Kosinski, 2022, 19:15) is not dubbed into the Hindi version. S&H green stamps were part of a customer incentive program popular in the second half of the twentieth century in the United States. The stamps could be traded for merchandise or redeemed for cash. This is a difficult culture specific reference to translate, as there is no equivalent in the target culture. The cultural weightage of "S&H green stamps" (Balda, 2022, 10:48) is lost when dubbed to "rang birangi stamp". Similarly, pet rock is a popular toy from the mid-70s that does not have an equivalent in the target culture. "Pet rock" (Balda, 2022, 31:30) has been dubbed as "do kaudikepatthar", thereby eliminating the cultural reference of the source.

The strategy of Loan is used in "Bullseye" (Kosinski, 2022, 01:22:18) as it is dubbed as "Bullseye". This phrase does not have the same currency in the target culture as the source culture, yet the translator chose to loan the phrase from the source. This might be because of the paucity of time in the dialogue. A similar strategy is used in "Frampton Comes Alive!" (Balda, 2022, 26:33) and "Gesundheit!" (Balda, 2022, 58:01) when these are borrowed as "Frampton Comes Alive!" and "Gesundheit!" in the Hindi dubbed version. In the above examples, while there does not seem to be a constraint on the time, the translator chose to retain the source phrases in dubbing.

An example of losing the impact of the verbal utterance can be found in the idiomatic expression "Oh for crying out loud" (Balda, 2022, 05:01) dubbed to "bahut hogayachillana". The source phrase is used to express annoyance or frustration. Wild Knuckles, one of the supervillains from the group Vicious six is frustrated that deadly tchotchkes try to kill him. In this context, in frustration, he exclaims "Oh for crying out loud". This feeling is not transferred to the target through the above dubbed expression in Hindi. A similar strategy is used in "Oh, you've got to be kidding me!" (Kosinski, 2022, 22:12) when it is dubbed as "yeh koi sapnathonahin".

Explication is a strategy that is used in instances where the dubbing is not constrained by technical limitations like temporality of the dialogue. For example, "For reasons known only to the Almighty and your guardian angel" (Kosinski, 2022, 17:31) is dubbed as "ooparvaale ne tumhaarekiyekuchhchunindaachchhekarmonkeevajah se". The addition of "acchekamomkeevajah se" results in an allusion that Maverick is lucky that his service is not terminated. The source phrase has this allusion built into it.

Analysis of a total of 85 cultural references in both films indicates that substitution is the most used strategy in dubbing the films *Top Gun: Maverick* and *Minions: The Rise of Gru* fromEnglish to Hindi. 76% of the culture specific references were dubbed using substitution in *Top Gun: Maverick* and 73% in *Minions: The Rise of Gru.*

Conclusion

Substitution of the source culture specific reference with a reference that is closer to the target culture is the most used translation strategy in dubbing the films *Top Gun: Maverick* and *Minions: The rise of Gru.* The difference in the target demographic of these two films does not impact the most common strategy used in dubbing. With most of the culture specific references being substituted by references from the target culture, a high level of domestication has been achieved in the case of dubbing the films mentioned above. Further studies involving multitudinous films and their corresponding Hindi dubbed versions will help corroborate the current study's findings. Studies spanning various related Indian languages can help identify and bring forward generalisations related to dubbing at the level of a language group.

References

1. Balda, K. (Director). (2022). Minions: The Rise of Gru [Film].Illumination Entertainment.
2. Chaume, F. (2020). Dubbing. In Bogucki, L., &Deckert, M. (Eds.), *The Palgrave handbook of Audiovisual translation and media accessibility*(1st ed.). Springer Nature.
3. Chiaro, D. (2012). Audiovisual Translation. In Chapelle, C. A. (Ed.), *The Encyclopedia of Applied Linguistics*. Wiley.
4. Díaz Cintas, J. (2009). Introduction – Audiovisual Translation: An Overview
5. of its Potential. In Diaz-Cintas, J. (Ed.), *New Trends in Audiovisual Translation* (pp. 1-20). Bristol, England: Multilingual Matters.
6. Kosinski, J. (Director). (2022). *Top Gun: Maverick* [Film]. Paramount Pictures.

7. Pérez-González, L. (2014). *Audiovisual translation.* London, England: Routledge.

8. Ranzato, I. (2016). *Translating culture specific references on television: The case of dubbing.* Routledge.

9. Sharma, A. (2019, July 5). Indians would rather watch content with subtitles than dubbed versions: Survey. *Mint.* https://www.livemint.com/industry/media/indians-would-rather-watch-content-with-subtitles-than-dubbed-versions-survey-1562327711012.html.

CHAPTER V

Role Of Anime And Manga Industries In Propagating Japanese Nationalism

Dibakar De, Research Scholar, Amity Institute of International Studies, Amity University Uttar Pradesh, Noida.

Dr Monish Tourangbam,Assistant Professor III, Ph.D. Coordinator and Programme Leader. Amity Institute of International Studies, Amity University Uttar Pradesh, Noida.

Role of Anime and Manga Industries in Propagating Japanese Nationalism

Abstract

Japanese nationalism has been widely scrutinized and disputed throughout Asia and within Japan in the years following World War II; in order to comprehend its position in Japan today, it is vital to understand what "Japanese nationalism" means. An incident in 2001 involving a North Korean spy vessel was deemed as a landmark in Japan's post-war history as its first assertive move in decades, marking a sharp contrast in its past incursions when it had last sunk a foreign vessel near the end of the 2nd World War. Even a decade ago in the 90s, would have this kind of behaviour by the Japanese been deemed as improbable. Tokyo's apparent willingness to use force indicated a significant transition in how the Japanese had started viewing their nation and its defensive capabilities.Presently however, the situation is started to alter itself; with this kind of sentiment trickling down from government circles to the public sphere where Japanese residents have gradually been receiving exposure to nationalist thoughts and deliberations, leading to a widespread belief amongst them, in Japan's ability to surpass every country in the world while upholding a unique identity. The economic might of Japan has served as a catalyst to the aforementioned unique identity wherein the advances in Japanese technology, financial sector and the entertainment industry had taken the world by awe and admiration.Multi-dimensional success in the fields of automobiles, banking, education, robotics & scientific innovation as well as mass media, led to it becoming one of the most – if not the most – intriguing countries in the world, resulting into the divergence from just hard power to soft power projection.The development of national pride among its citizens in the years between the 1980s and mid-1990s culminated into the re-emergence of Japanese nationalism, but with a much more different shade than its previous iteration. The factor that set apart this new nationalism from the older one was the methodology and tools used by the Japanese government in the attempt to meet its objectives. This paper aims to explore one of the instruments that has been widely put to use by Japan in this regard: the Anime and Manga industries. Anime and Manga are two different platforms of storytelling media, both of which originate in Japan.By observing the multitude of themes present in these platforms, a correlation between the Anime and Manga industry and sentiments of nationalism. Studies have revealed the effects of these industries world over: rising artistic freedom to comment over global phenomena in Japan and increase in the level of respect, admiration and genuine interest in the country's society and history by citizens from all walks of life across the planet.In approximately four decades since the end of the World War II, Japan had gone from being on the extreme negative end of the spectrum of likeability of a country to being on the most positive end of it.

Introduction

Japanese nationalism has been widely scrutinized and disputed throughout Asia and within Japan in the years following World War II; in order to comprehend its position in Japan today, it is vital to understand what "Japanese nationalism" means. Historians follow the Tokugawa era, which started in 1603, but it wasn't until the Meiji era (1868–1922) that the world witnessed the emergence of Japanese nationalism. Taking into its contemporary shape as a fascist-inspired philosophy, likewise, as a movement that would result in instability across the world and the region. Nationalism was marginalised in Japan's public discourse after 1945—at least until recently. This exclusion was brought on by Japan's "fear of itself," in large part. This psychological syndrome was driven by memories of the humiliating Japanese high command's surrender to the US forces as well as the catastrophic effects of the nuclear bombs delivered on Hiroshima and Nagasaki. Two main worries trigger the fear: first, that if Japan's military is granted excessive authority, it would once more inflict the nation immense suffering; and second, that the Japanese people themselves might once more support militarism. Article 9 of the country's American-drafted constitution, which essentially pledges it to pacifism, ensures its ardent antinuclear stance, and makes it difficult for the nation to really provide military support to its allies, has been subject to critical scrutiny in the recent few years. Japanese officials thus far, have opposed the nation's rearmament for the majority of the last 77 years because of their fear of themselves and not out of a selfish desire to avoid the expense of keeping a modern standing army, as otherwise claimed by certain entities. Presently however, the situation is started to alter itself; with this kind of sentiment trickling down from government circles to the public sphere where Japanese residents have gradually been receiving exposure to nationalist thoughts and deliberations, leading to a widespread belief amongst them, in Japan's ability to surpass every country in the world while upholding a unique identity.

Rationale of The Study

The economic might of Japan has served as a catalyst to the aforementioned unique identity wherein the advances in Japanese technology, financial sector and the entertainment industry had taken the world by awe and admiration. After the 2nd World War, the numbness post defeat and occupation were gradually replaced by self-assurance and a new type of nationalism within the Japanese people, which was inspired by the notion that their country, is the economic powerhouse of East Asia. It can be said without a doubt that Japan is getting ready to resume playing a more active—and independent—role in world events after decades of adopting a passive stance and withdrawal from major power contests in Asia. Given the gradual rise of a dominant China since the last twenty years, which shares close geopolitical proximity with the island nation and the onset of a Great Power competition with the U.S., Japan's security guarantor for all these years, the country has been left with little choice but to return from a prolonged self-imposed exile away from assertive politics.Multi-dimensional success in the fields of automobiles, banking, education, robotics & scientific innovation as well as mass media, led to it becoming one of the most – if not the most – intriguing countriesin the world, resulting into the divergence from just hard power to soft powerprojection. The development of national pride among its citizens in the years between the 1980s and mid-1990s culminated into the re-emergence of Japanese nationalism, but with a much more different shade than its previous iteration. The factor that set apart this new nationalism from the older one was the methodology and tools used by Japan in the attempt to meet its objectives; Nation-Branding is one such instrument in this regard. This paper aims to explore the activity of Nation-Branding carried out by leveraging two platforms in this regard: the Anime and Manga industries. Anime and Manga are two different platforms of storytelling media, both of which originate in Japan.By observing the multitude of themes present in these platforms, a correlation between the Anime and Manga industry and sentiments of nationalism. Studies have revealed the effects of these industries world over: rising artistic freedom to comment over global phenomena in Japan and increase in the level of respect, admiration and genuine interest in the country's society and history by citizens from all walks of life across the planet.In approximately four decades since the end of the World War II, Japan had gone from being on the extreme negative end of the spectrum of likeability of a country to being on the most positive end of it.

Literature Review

Cool Japan Initiative and Japanese Nation Branding

The concept and practice of Nation-Branding has gained a considerable amount of traction in recent years; an increasing number of governments across the international arena have begun utilising techniques within the ambit of commercial branding to enhance their respective country's image and reputation that overlaps a wide array of sectors. Japan's efforts to attract inward investment, which is often one of the main goalswithin Nation-Branding strategies, have piqued global interest along with its government's strong involvement in establishing and strengthening initiatives to increase the country's exports and tourism.The Japanese government has committed to implementing policies that promote popular Japanese culture such as anime, manga, games, music and fashion in order to give rise to the increasingly accepted notion of the"Cool Japan" policy. The emergence of this particular policy has in turn led to the development of the"Cool Japan Craze"which refers to the policy competition in which many of the central ministries have decided to engage in with increased proactiveness. The idea behind escalating "Cool Japan" involves boosting Japan's content industry which serves as a driving force for the commercial sector of the nation, thereby enriching Japanese "Soft Power" (Nye, Joseph, 1990). The ripples generated as a consequence of these developments have been felt across the international community, for example, in a 2002 essay for Foreign Policy headlined "Japan's Gross National Cool," Douglas McGray described Japan as a "reinventing superpower" that was growing its cultural impact abroad despite the political and economic difficulties of the "Lost Decade."McGray examined the influences on youth culture, including J-pop, manga, anime, video games, fashion, film, consumer electronics, architecture, cuisine, and kawaii ("cuteness") phenomena like Hello Kitty. He also emphasised Japan's significant cultural soft power, raising the question of what message the nation might wish to convey.With the theoretical foundation provided by this "Cool Japan" concept, the government began to promote the idea of "cultural diplomacy" through well-known cultural items and maintained that the content industry might become the new leading sector of the Japanese economy (METI 2005; The Council for the Asian Gateway Initiative 2007a; Condry 2009).In its cultural diplomacy, the Ministry of Foreign Affairs, for instance, currently favours using manga, anime, and popular music in addition to high culture like flower arranging and kabuki (classical dance-drama).

After the "Cool Japan" phrase was coined by McGray in 2002, the notion itself was endorsed by the US, whose popular culture has had a considerable amount of impact on the Japanese society till date after their defeat in World War II. While American cultural influence prevailed in Japan with the help of mass media, it started to decrease from the 1970s (Matsui, 2014). Having transformed into a prosperous society by amalgamating various western cultural attributes to its own, Japanese popular culture witnessed a substantial growth and increase in attractiveness. American popular culture slowly waned from having a dominating influence on the nation as observed during the 1980s, Japanese economic supremacy was hailed and its reverence of the US dissolvedconcurrently. Although the bubble burst of the Japanese economy had a devastating impact on the self-confidence of the nation as a whole as a result of losing in the economic rivalry with other countries prevalent at the time, giving more emphasis to the "Lost Decade" phrase, Japan's efforts in building its national identity through nation branding practices paid off not too long after the burst. Japanese confidence was restored by reports of the success of Japanese cultural products. Names like Nintendo, PlayStation, Hello Kitty, Pokémon, and Tamagotchi entered both the Japanese-speaking world and the daily lives of youngsters. The majority of children's programming on US cable television is today comprised of Japanese anime-style animations, and Pokémon even graced the cover of Time magazine (McGray 2002, Nikkei Business 2005). Subsequently, McGray's 2002 essay on Japan's Gross National Cool sparked a surge of cultural nationalism within the society.

Anime& Manga and Japanese Nationalism

Nationalism is a deep feeling of attachment to a homeland and absolute loyalty to it, along with a shared sense of destiny of a people due to their common ethnicity or race (Kohn, 1944). National identity on the other hand, is the means by which a culture is defined through a vast collection of individuals who share subjective feelings and resonance with each other about a nation. If an individual or a group of individuals display their national identity, it is considered to be akin to patriotism and taking pride in one's own nation, achieving nationalism. Historically, different groups have displayed this sort of sentiment using a multitude of cultural and ethnic mannerisms; examples include Ancient Greek sculptures, philosophical texts and general involvement in intellectual avenues, Ancient Roman Gladiatorial shows, engineering marvels and their belief in the hierarchic system (Nielsen, 1999), Spanish Flamenco dance and Bull Fighting, the British Empire's propagation of the English language, Chinese Taoism, martial arts and mathematic prowess and last but not least, India as a land of spirituality, various architectural marvels and artistic wonders.

In a similar fashion, Japan too, had displayed its nationalism using imperial militarism in the past. It is only very recently, since the last few decades, that Japan has adopted an entirely different method for promoting its societal and cultural heritage. After its many economic, military, demographic, and political transitionsin the years beyond World War II and the years beyond that, the country decided to embark upon a journey of reinventing itself as a new kind of superpower. Post 1970s, Japan's global cultural influence has grown quietly and steadily; from automobiles to unique electronic goods to architecture to cuisine to even behavioural mannerisms, the country has evolved from being just an economic superpower in the 1980s to being a cultural superpower as well, in the present.Nationalism is defined as a political principle holding that the political and national unit should be congruent, as a sentiment about that principle, and as a theory of political legitimacy requiring that ethnic boundaries should not cut across political ones (Inoguchi, 2015). From this statement, it is possible to connect the idea to the notion of *Nihonjinron* which essentially denotes "discourse of the Japanese" and aims to situate Japan as an ethnically homogenous and unified society especially in the Post War period.Nihonjinron is defined as a form of cultural nationalism that aims to regenerate national community in creating, preserving or strengthening a people's cultural identity when it is felt to be lacking, inadequate or threatened. By associating specific political and social conditions that the ruling group wants with the idea of an unbroken imperial dynasty, Nihonjinron legitimises these conditions. As a result, Nihonjinron continues to play a key role in discussions about nationalism in Japanese culture and film as well as in politics of representation (Ko 2010). Anime and Manga are two platforms of media, both of which originate in Japan. It has been observed that anime has been profoundly influenced by Western designs, particularly the original works of Walt Disney. Like Anime, the 'Manga' has had a similar point of origin and is commonly viewed as "graphic novels" or comic books; although these terms do very little justice to explaining the nature of the message and information contained within this platform. Unlike Anime, Manga has already existed for nearly four centuries, dating back to at least the Tokugawa period in the 1600s, when woodblock prints were used to tell various kinds of stories and attracted people from all ages, elite and common circles.

The platform of Anime as we know it at present, witnessed its emergence in 1963, at the hands of the famed Osamu Tezuka, who was the creator of the world's first anime, *Astro Boy* while the Manga of the same name had begun being published in 1952, merely seven years after World War II. Soon after, many more such projects underwent development and after their release, became instant hits with the eagerly awaiting public. One of the most famous Anime films to have ever been released is *Grave of the Fireflies* which showcased the tragedies that ensued in the aftermath of the World War II and made immense contributions in raising awareness about the consequences of pursuing an aggressive military policy in the first place, a notion that strengthened Japan's severe reluctance to possess an active military and nuclear artillery well into the 2020s.Anime is now viewed as the true window to the global audience for gaining awareness about the multifaceted and enthralling Japanese visual culture as well as society.Over the years, both Anime and Manga have been connected to various aspects of Japanese society including the school system, education, family structure, architecture, religious and ethnic customs and psychological health. The cultural impact of Manga on the Japanese society can be perceived in both negative and positive light; the platform has often been used to offer a discourse on the perceptions of the human world on religion, behavioural patterns, sexuality, violence, and psychological development. This has frequently led it to coming under harsh condemnation by a few countries due the sensitive nature of the subject matter discussed; these countries see the medium of Japanese Manga as an indirect assault on their cultural belief systems (Mahaseth, 2018).

Nationalism and Japanese animation as well as manga have a long history of being associated with each other. Even before anime was created, other forms of animation were employed in Japan to foster a sense of nationalism. *Kokka Kimigayo* (The National Anthem: His Majesty's Reign, 1931), an animated short produced by OfujiNoburo, was likely one of the most frequently viewed works of domestic animation in the 1930s since it was used to encourage the singing of Japan's national anthem before movie screenings. (Clements, 2013). Developing on this early corelationbetween Japanese animation and nationalism, World War II saw the implementationof cinematic animated films for propaganda both inside and outside of Japan (Cohen, 1997). The linkages between Japanese animation and nationalism emerged at this time; the *Momotaro* films (Seo Mitsuyo, 1945 and 1947), which served as wartime propaganda, served as the country's first attempts at producing feature-length cel animation. Since then, anime has evolved into a conduit with a complex history of national identity being represented in the form of both nationalism and statelessness (Napier, 2005).

The visual and cultural prowess of Japan can be linked to its identity as a state in the sense that both these dimensions are not independent of each other, but rather supportive. The notion of American cultural influence in the Japanese society fading away from a dominant position has been said to have fashioned a feeling of insecurity within the United States, leading to the term "Japanization" being coined. This phenomenon involves the American citizens increasingly becoming accustomed to utilizing products of Japanese origin, ranging from food ingredients to consumer electronics to clothes to automobiles and to even entertainment sources. This fear stems from the shared uneasiness amongst American policy makers with regard to losing national influence over most global affairs which would be followed by the United States being walled out of its self-created mechanism of earning financial and political dividends from other states. So great was the American insecurity that when Anime episodes would be broadcast in the US in the late 1980s, the editors and directors would resort to stripping away all visual and plot references to Japan and instead Americanize them in their entirety (McKevitt, 2010). This case of American insecurity has further been exacerbated through the direct portrayal of right-wing nationalist sentiments,attacking both present day Japanese politics and historical documentations of the same,in certain Anime series that have been broadcast internationally. A particular Anime series *"GATE"* can be cited as an example in this aspect; this series has taken various tropes to comment upon the aforementioned right-wing nationalist themes. The series takes note of the sense of shame felt by the Japanese about having to undeniably rely upon the United States as their security guarantor, and attempts to alter it by portraying the mass killings of US military personnel in its episodes. *"GATE"*further attempts to squash the existing critics of Japanese military behaviour by putting the blame upon "feminization" of the country's politics; moreover, iconic scenes from US-Vietnam war films have been remade into US-Japanese scenes (Hernandez et. al, 2018).

Research Objectives

- To identify and locate a new form of Japanese nationalism within Anime and Manga.
- To analyse the interlinkages between Japan's cultural diplomacy and soft power.

Research Questions

- How does Japan utilise the Anime and Manga Industries to propagate its culture and heritage?
- Do these platforms play an extended role in reflecting Japan's aspirations as a major political power?
- How have the Anime and Manga Industries been used as tools to divert attention from Japan's past political and military endeavours?

Research Methodology

The aim of this research is to establish a correlation between the Anime and Manga industry and Japanese nationalism and to observe whether these avenues play an extended role in securing Japan's future as a political as well as military power. The reason behind the choice of the theme stems from notion that within these platforms, the Japanese society is often portrayed on top of a pedestal, where Japan is essentially shown to have an international standing similar to that of the United States and other major powers. Qualitative Analysisshall be the main research tool utilised.

Findings and Analysis

With respect to the first research question, it can be agreed upon with certainty that Anime and Manga have served as definite platforms for enabling the cultural output of Japan. Japanese animation is incredibly infused with national culture and contagious. Japan has also been Asia's first cultural exporter with the aid of anime culture; in fact, it has been declared as Japan's greatest cultural export (Saito, 2007). In Japan, animation has grown into a vital economic sector, and the country's development strategy is rich in cultural traditions and national features, ensuring the sustainability of the industry's growth. While focusing on upholding its own national features and customs, Japanese culture is both open and closed, meaning it is adept at assimilating the superior cultures of other countries. This cultural trait is also mirrored in Japanese animation, which explores the exotic essence of culture while simultaneously carrying forward domestic culture.The culture of food that anime has introduced is one of the many ways that Japanese heritage has been assimilated into other parts of the world. Millions of videos with the hashtag *"#animefood"* may be found on apps such as Instagram and TikTok with a quick search. In these videos, individuals are shown recreating stunning Japanese cuisine seen in various anime series. Foods like Ramen, Onigiri, and Cold Soba Noodles are featured within this hashtag, which has had over 500 million views.

The second research question pertains to anime and manga serving as a window into Japan's political and military behaviour. Japanese animation has had multiple phases throughout the years; from the 1960s to 1980s, storylines of multiple anime series focused on the hardships of war, consequences of pursuing aggressive militarism and the cost of advancements in nuclear technology (eg: *Astro Boy, Grave of the Fireflies, Gojira etc.)*. Subsequently as Japan's economic might started expanding from the 1970s to early 1990s, anime and manga storylines also started reflecting the transformations surging through its society, whereby most of the plots displayed Japan as either a technologically futuristic society or Japanese characters being indispensable in comparison to characters of other nationalities, especially those from the Western powers (eg: *Wicked City, City Hunter, Cyber City Oedo, Fist of the North Star etc.)*. Post 1990s, after the burst of the economic bubble, Japan had already realised the far reach of soft power, further highlighted by the birth of the 'Cool Japan' concept. Anime and Manga series now shifted their focus away from the political and military past of the nation and the apologetic undertones that could once be observed, had started fading away. Since the beginning of this period, there have been multiple anime series as well as manga publications which explore plots in which Japan has been shown to either be a leading military force with an authoritarian institution in force, or the nation is actively involved in overseas military operations, in which even US military forces are rendered subservient to the Japanese. This type of portrayal seems to be directly hinting at the underlying political aspirations of Japan as a member of the international community. Examples of these anime series are: *Code Geass, Gundam, GATE, Death Note*etc. The *Momotaro* films during the World War II can also be looked upon as having had served as a predecessor for portraying Japanese military prowess and awakening nationalistic sentiments within the wider scope of the society.

The third research question is concerned with how Anime and Manga have served as tools which have altered the perceptions of international audiences as well as governments towards itself throughout the years since the end of World War II. Essentially, both platforms have metamorphosed the country's global recognition as an imperialistic military empire to a pop-cultural superpower. The anime series and films released since the 1960s to the mid 1980s always carried apologetic overtones along with narratives vehemently discouraging violence and war, as a homage to the immense casualties experienced during the end of World War II.Moving forward to the 90s and then 2000s, when the Cool Japan thesis had already been established and Japanese soft power realised, American and other Western audiences experienced a paradigm shift in their perspectives on the East Asian country; Japan was now viewed as a sort of fantasyland, the creator of popular Manga comics, home to the giant gaming industry, land of Anime and a glamourous tourist destination. In the span of a few decades, Japan's global image had altered drastically; transmuting from a fearsome enemy and upholder of evil to a producer of automobiles, robotics and a country with aningenious creative fantasy factor attached to it.

Conclusion

It is without a doubt that Anime and Manga have functioned as near perfect conduits for propagating Japanese cultural influence within the international arena and thereby amassing a vast amount of Soft Power in its arsenal. Over the years since the end of World War II, Japan managed to completely shift its national identity from that of an atrocious aggressor to that of a sophisticated and ingenuous land of marvel and fantasy. The emergence of the Cool Japan notion and it eventually becoming part of the Japanese government's official policy wherein, the idea that Anime and Manga have been the nation's greatest cultural export, are examples of the birth of a new Japanese national identity, contrasting its past. Anime has acted as a channel for the spread of *Nihonjinron*, a concept which aims to explore, analyse and explain the many peculiarities of Japanese culture and mentality by comparing it to that of Europe and North America. These platforms are considered to be culturally malleable, which is why they have been able to economically promote cross-border influence. Creators of respective Anime and Manga series have often indubitably used them as tools to comment upon long-standing and ongoing aspects of the world. The existence of series which constantly show extensive imagery of the Japanese outsmarting foreign nations or the righteousness and benevolence of Japan in comparison to the rest of the world, is a signal towards nationalism within the Japanese society stirring up at a rapid pace. While it may not directly translate to nationalistic sentiments being generated within the viewers immediately, there certainly is a heavy impact of normalizing depictions of Japanese militarisation and overall superiority, upon those who already share these nationalist ideals.

References

1. Denison, Rayna. (2018). Anime's Cultural Nationalism: The Politics of Representing Japan in Summer Wars (Mamoru Hosoda, 2009). Mutual Images Journal. 123-142. 10.32926/2018.5.den.anime.

2. Josephy-Hernández, Daniel E. & Rivera-Marín, Jorge & Tomita, Ai. (2019). (2019) New Japanese Nationalism in Anime.

3. Cabrera, Nicole. (2016). Japanese Nationalism In Manga マンガに見られるナショナリズム. Furman University, Greenville SC.

4. Mahaseth, Harsh. (2018). The Cultural Impact of Manga on Society. 1-5. 10.9734/AJL2C/2018/45673.

5. MCKEVITT, A. (2010). "You Are Not Alone!": Anime and the Globalizing of America. *Diplomatic History*, *34*(5), 893-921. Retrieved August 15, 2021, from http://www.jstor.org/stable/24916463.

6. Darum, M., 2021. *The Evolution of Japan in the face of Anime and Manga.* [online] Iapss.org. Available at: <https://www.iapss.org/2014/05/15/from-militarism-to-media-the-evolution-of-japanese-nationalism-in-the-face-of-anime-and-manga/> [Accessed 15 August 2021].

7. Tamogami, "Was Japan an Aggressor Nation?", p. 1.

8. Penney, M. P. (2009). Nationalism and Anti-Americanism in Japan – Manga Wars, Aso, Tamogami, and Progressive Alternatives. *The Asia-Pacific Journal,* *7*(17). https://apjjf.org/-Matthew-Penney/3116/article.pdf

9. Ko, Mika (2010).Nihonjinron: The ideology of Japaneseness. *Routledge.*

10. Clements, Jonathan (2013). Anime: A History. *British Film Institute.* 9781844573905 (ISBN10: 1844573907)

11. Cohen, K.F. (1997) Forbidden Animation: Censored Cartoons and Blacklisted Animators in America. Jefferson: McFarland and Co

12. Inoguchi, T. (2015) National Identity and Adapting to Integration: Nationalism and Globalization in Japan. In: Suryadinata, L., ed. Nationalism and Globalization. Singapore: ISEAS-Yusof Ishak Institute, 215- 233.

13. Ko, M. (2010) Japanese Cinema and Otherness: Nationalism, Multiculturalism and the Problem of Japaneseness. London: Routledge.

14. McGray, D. (2009) Japan's Gross National Cool. Foreign Policy [Online], 11 November. Available from: https://foreignpolicy.com/2009/11/11/japans-gross-national-cool.

15. Napier, S.J. (2005) Anime from Akira to Howl's Moving Castle: Experiencing Contemporary Japanese Animation. Basingstoke: Palgrave

16. Matsui, T. (2014). NATION BRANDING THROUGH STIGMATIZED POPULAR CULTURE: THE "COOL JAPAN" CRAZE AMONG CENTRAL MINISTRIES IN JAPAN. *Hitotsubashi Journal of Commerce and Management,* 48(1 (48)), 81–97. http://www.jstor.org/stable/43295053

OTT Consumption of Transnational Television Reruns and Fan Practices in India: A Case Study

Aakriti Kohli, Assistant Professor, Department of Journalism, Delhi College of Arts and Commerce, University of Delhi, Netaji Nagar, Delhi

Introduction

Consumption of popular television shows available as reruns on OTT platforms opens an exciting field of cultural enquiry into how these media texts are received, re-articulated and re-situated by audiences themselves. The global cultural economy in its transnational mode of operation is primarily influenced by and flows via the nodes of American cultural production. This paper takes the case study of reruns of a popular television sitcom, *Friends* which ran on NBC from 1994 to 2004, completing 10 seasons and 238 episodes, available for streaming on Netflix now. This paper makes use of online surveys and participant observation of online fan groups, and draws on theoretical works of Hill (2007) and Morley (1986) on television and pleasure, Jenkins (1992) and de Certeau (1984) on fan practices, Hall (1997) and Appadurai (1990) on global media culture, and Spigel (1995) and Kompare (2005) on television reruns to build a prism via which pleasures of transnational cultural modernity and consumption of television reruns on OTT and fan practices in India can be put in perspective. The central concerns of this paper include why and what do audiences seek in watching reruns of popular television shows? Is it because television programming which relies on tested television shows ensures high volume of audiences to be delivered to OTT platforms or do audiences themselves seek particular kinds of pleasure in watching reruns of their favorite shows? In essence, why do we watch what we watch? This requires an attempt to unravel the inherent logic of transnational television reruns of episodic narratives, the themes that make them timeless and the interrelated questions of cultural production and reception. This paper also delves into the phenomenon of fan practices around the show i.e. the second order of production (consumption) by way of which the audience receives, makes use of and interacts with the text. Subsequently this paper probes the level of active consumption by way of which fans may engage with a text, including recontextualization (where fans may add to the text's narrative and offer explanations), cross-overs (cross-referencing other television programmes and characters) and personalization (fans inserting themselves in the narrative). Towards the end this paper argues that a show such as *Friends* is a familiar space most audiences continue to return to, find relevant, seek comfort in, and identify with their life, not just as banal television but as a meaningful repository of love, relationships and friendship.

Previous research on television watching practices in the field of cultural studies has explored the element of pleasure in consuming television, discussing the problematic overt emphasis on pleasure (Hill, 2007) or the guilty-ridden pleasure of watching television itself (Morley, 1986). The act of watching television or televisual content may be conscious or unconscious, where audiences may or may not reflect on the television text as a purveyor of ideology. Subsequently audience engagement and mode of viewing a genre such as news and current affairs will be distinctly different from other genres such as situation comedies. Battles and Hilton–Morrow (2002), for instance, argue that situation comedies rarely deal with political issues and largely depend on interpersonal relationships and individuated acts to pull the narrative forward. In that sense audience expectation from situation comedies will tend to be different from other television genres. Popular psychology reports from a study conducted in 2012 suggest that watching reruns of our favorite television shows may boost our will power and may have restorative powers (McGonigal, 2012). As per the report, the participants in the study who were asked to write about their favorite shows performed better at structured tasks than those who were asked to list items in their room. The researchers concluded that watching reruns had a "measurable restorative effect from a familiar fictional world."[1] Being a consumer of popular television shows has led me to think further on why and what do audiences seek in watching reruns of popular television shows available on OTT platforms. Is it because of television programming which relies on tested television shows to ensure high volume of audiences to be delivered to advertisers or do audiences themselves seek particular kinds of pleasure in watching reruns of their favorite shows? Why do we watch what we watch?

Transnational television content has been available in India from 1991 onwards via satellite, cable, direct-to-home and the Internet more recently.[2] Before the convenience of watching television shows online, the repertoire of English-language shows produced in the US and UK available in India on cable was limited. Some of the longest running and most popular English-language drama and sit-com shows in India include but are not limited to *Friends, How I Met Your Mother, Big Bang Theory, Baywatch, Sienfeld, Bold and Beautiful, Sex and the City, Will & Grace, Dharma & Greg, Small Wonder* among others. In 2019 for instance, Netflix bought the rights for *Seinfeld's* 180 episodes for over $500 million (Horton, 2019).

India has never been a prominent exporter of transnational television content to international networks, barring Bollywood films. On the other hand, it has received much television content from the West. Chopra and Gajjala (2012) point out that transnational global media culture has inevitably brought to bear the concepts of concomitant cultural imperialism and homogenization of global culture in developing countries. However, some recent work on global media culture has been insightful in providing conceptual and theoretical maps of the complex spatial and temporal dynamics of media production, circulation and reception among audiences. Especially with reference to OTT, the production, circulation and proliferation of television media texts via global economy is an exciting field of cultural enquiry to understand how these media texts are received, re-articulated and re-situated by audiences themselves.

Reading the working of transnational media production practices into what Hall (1997, pp. 27) calls "global mass culture", one can understand the unbound nature of media content circulating globally today when he says that it is:

...dominated by the modern means of cultural production, dominated by the image which crosses and re-crosses linguistic frontiers much more rapidly and more easily, and which speaks across languages in a much more immediate way... by all the ways in which the visual and graphic arts have entered directly into the reconstitution of popular life, of entertainment and of leisure... by television and by film, and by the image, imagery, and styles of mass advertising. Its epitomy is in all those forms of mass communication of which one might think of satellite television as the prime example... its whole purpose is precisely that it cannot be limited any longer by national boundaries.

Arjun Appadurai (1990, pp. 299) on global cultural economy and transnational 'mediascapes' observes that they are,

...image-centered, narrative-based accounts of strips of reality, and what they offer to those who experience and transform them is a series of elements (such as characters, plots and textual forms) out of which scripts can be formed of imagined lives, their own as well as those of others living in other places.

The global cultural economy then in its transnational mode of operation is primarily influenced by and flows via the nodes of American cultural production. Kompare (2005) in his work tracing the historical emergence of reruns and repeat television in America remarks that a cultural and industrial history of reruns in the US points towards this phenomenon as a legitimate business practice in running of the television industry. He also goes on to argue that the format of repeat television in the US was to also construct a sense of national history and national past, something which is also discussed by Spigel (1995) in her work on popular memory and its negotiation with official historical past where televized heritage comes to stand in for heritage itself fostering particular notions of gender, class, race and ethnicity albeit in a teleological fashion.

Kompare further argues that television reruns should be seen as commoditized objects circulating in capitalist economies of cultural production thereby referring to the monetization of syndicated content, advertising revenues and a pre-tested and adapted audience for those programs. While this does explain the business logic of scheduling reruns of old television content as well as their availability now on OTT, however it does not adequately explain the continued patronage, engagement and consumption of reruns by the audiences themselves. More specifically it does not sufficiently throw light on how transnational television content and its reruns find resonance with viewers in a country like India, long after the show has stopped running or the continued fan engagement and concomitant fan practices around certain shows. This requires an attempt to unravel the inherent logic of transnational television reruns of episodic narratives, the themes that make them timeless and the interrelated questions of cultural production and reception.

My query with respect to reruns of popular television shows is specifically to do with the American sitcom *Friends* which ran on NBC from 1994 to 2004, completing 10 seasons and 238 episodes. The show follows the everyday professional and love lives of six friends in their 20s living in Manhattan, New York. Each character is sketched with particular quirks such as the "control freak" chef, the "dumb but good-looking" actor, the "waitress obsessed with her looks", the "nerdy paleontologist", the "witty corporate cog" and the "free-spirited masseuse and singer". These characters are essentially performing as young people carrying out modern day professions in one of the most expensive cities in the world.

From New York to New Delhi

It has been more than 20 years since the show aired on television but according to the Broadcast Audience Research Council in India between January and June 2016, the show aired on Viacom 18's Comedy Central (English entertainment channel), had 2.08 million impressions (Sathe 2012)[3]. Every few years there are rumors of the cast reuniting for another season or the release of the trailer of the film based on the show.[4]

The sitcom works on syndication, and generates $1 billion in syndication revenue for the Warner Bros every year and the cast of the show makes 2% of the syndication revenue each year as syndication royalties.[5] In 2002, NBC negotiated to renew the show for its last season, and are reported to have paid each member of the cast $1 million per episode for the last season.[6] In 2002 the show was doing 24.7 million viewers per week, with a 12 rating with adults between the ages of 18 and 49 making these numbers. The sitcom made use of many revenue channels, including the first-run ad revenues, broadcasting syndication and DVD sales. While no current DVD sales revenue figures have been released, a report indicates that in 2003 2.1 million copies of *Friends* DVDs were sold for $75 million.[7]

The show's rights were acquired by Romedy Now (an English-language television channel that broadcasts romantic comedies (American television shows and Hollywood films))in 2014 and ran for a few months after which the rights were also acquired by Comedy Central, which continues to broadcast the show in India. The show has previously run on Star World and Zee Café (English-language television channels that broadcast syndicated popular American television shows), sometimes simultaneously, with both channels showing different seasons. The content head for Romedy Now defends their decision to acquire the old sitcom on the premise that it fits well within their "love and laughter" motto, additionally the programme scheduling is done in such a way that individual episodes can be watched every night of the week from Monday to Thursday and "binge-watched" on Saturday in a marathon session.[8] The show also finds its audience not just on television but also on free online streaming websites and subscription-only portals such as Netflix, an online Video-on-Demand or OTT streaming website which bought the rights for streaming *Friends* for $500,000 per episodein 2015.[9] The show was briefly discontinued on Netflix after its rights were bought by Warner Media, however it has been back on the Netflix platform since 2020. While Netflix does not divulge the number of subscribers streaming a show or their viewing patterns but a Netflix spokesperson has been quoted as saying that *Friends* draws as much online buzz as other contemporary shows about young adults.[10]As per a report, approximately 32 million minutes of *Friends* has been streamed on Netflix as on December 2019 (Vyotko, 2019).

The show, with its emphasis on the individual in a society, the hopes and ambitions, the individual struggles and challenges, is aspirational when it comes to living on your own, pursuing your dreams, dating woes etc. The characters do not engage with their immediate political environment, where current events only come in passing as a reference to a joke. Socio-economic issues are the individual's alone who must triumph over them to be a part of the society. The show is a capitalist dream – a new vacation, a new car, a new job, a new piece of jewelry, new-found love, all of these are the lampposts of high points in the character's lives. All the characters in the show are heterosexual (barring comic references to one of the character's father who is gay and performs in drag) and white.

The emerging question is that how can a show that aired in 1994 and ran till 2004 still continues to find relevance among audiences in India? A similar thought is articulated by Sternbergh (2016, p. 4) who observes:

The world of *Friends* is notable, to modern eyes, for what it encompasses about being young and single and carefree in the city but also for what it doesn't encompass: social media, smartphones, student debt, the sexual politics of Tinder, moving back in with your parents as a matter of course, and a national mood that vacillates between anxiety and defeatism.

The Cultural Economy of Repetition on OTT

Where does then *Friends* fit into the current lives of the youth and more specifically where does it fit in the current lives of Indian youth who are watching it for the first time and/or watching the reruns on OTT? Taking off from this question I began having preliminary discussions with my students about the show, their personal memory of watching it for the first time and their practices associated with the show. For many of my undergraduate media students in the ages of 18 and 21, their popular memory and memorialization around the show leads them to believe that it was perhaps their first brush with all things modern and progressive or all things American specifically. Even for my generation, those who were born in the mid-1980s, the show for us was a commencement of young adult life and independent decision-making, albeit with a dose of everyday humor. Subsequent discussions with my students regarding their television viewing habits led me to search for a community of audiences who still watched the show and continued to engage with it. Since I was looking for new and old audiences, I searched for online groups dedicated to the show. I found a group specifically for Indian fans of the show on a popular social networking website (Facebook) with over 87,000 members. It was a closed group and I had to send in a formal request for joining in. The description of the group reads as "Great TV Show which gets more funnier (sic) each time you see when not in great mood. Do watch any episode it really makes your day and you become friends to the characters in the even though you don't know them personally." For the purpose of this research, I adopted the methodology of an online qualitative and quantitative survey along with online participant observation of the group community to study individual fan behavior and inter-personal fan practices.

Before carrying out the survey I wrote a time-bound post in the group in May 2020 asking interested members to write to me about their experience of watching the show and if they would be interested in taking part in the study. I received 87 messages from members who were interested in talking about the show and demonstrated interest in taking part in the study. After an exchange of messages about the show, their memories of it and their continued engagement with it, I emailed the survey to them. Out of the total 87, 83 members completed the survey. My respondents were both male and female, between the ages of 17 and 38, living in metropolitan cities of India. Most of the respondents remember watching their first episode of the show when they were anywhere between 12 to 14 years of age on Netflix (OTT) (42%), television (40%) and on DVD (2%). On television, the respondents recalled watching the show on Star World and Comedy Central in equal numbers, followed by Zee Café. 94% of the respondents admitted to still watching the show on a regular basis, with 55% watching it on television. During the initial interview exchange, some respondents admitted that they come across the show while surfing channels and do not specifically seek out the show during its scheduled hours. About 59% of the respondents said that they specially streamed the show on Netflix.

The show came to an end in 2004 and Netflix and Comedy Central has been running different seasons and episodes multiple times during the year, this is also evident from 88% of the respondents who claim that they have watched some episodes more than 5 times. Each episode is roughly

22 minutes, with 8 minutes of commercial break.While television (cable networks/DTH) continues to dominate as the medium of preference for watching all kinds of televisual content, 57% of the respondents used Video-On-Demand and online streaming services such as Netflix, Hotstar and Amazon Prime (Netflix, Amazon Prime and Hotstar are paywalled online streaming platforms which offer watching of television shows and films on their platform for a fee. Hotstar in an Indian platform whereas Netflix and Amazon Prime are international services). Revealingly 90% of the respondents admitted to watching television shows online (which may also include illegal and pirated streaming websites). 73% of the respondents admitted to streaming *Friends* episodes online, suggesting that it's not just programming of reruns on television but also voluntary seeking out of old episodes online for viewing.

In some of the detailed descriptions on why they like the show, the respondents explain the characters, humour, relatable situations, and context of the show, which has an undying appeal for them. Some responses also described the uniqueness of each character and the building of a relationship with the characters after all these years. Some respondents also admitted to knowing the characters like their own friends and predicting how the characters will respond in a given situation. The show continues to be an important reference point even now for many of them.Many pointed out to the nonchalance with which the characters dealt with important life decisions and issues such as marriage, divorce, job loss, childlessness and dating failures. As one young female respondent said: "The show tells you to take life easy...*Friends* is easy on the head, not too complex and always funny."Some of the respondents (9 females and 5 males) also shared that watching reruns of episodes they have seen before is reassuring, and the concerns and issues of the characters continue to find relevance in their life as well. Even though the show speaks of the American way of living, some of the cultural practices and issues finding prominence in the show such as finding a dream job, throwing a get-together, retail-therapy to address mood swings, dating troubles, falling in and out of love, resonate with them at a personal level, and consequent identification with the characters bringing them back to the show.

An overarching observation by women respondents was about how the show has had an impact on the way they dressed, and specially their hairstyle. A running joke in the show is one of the character's overweight days when she was young and the constant fat-shaming that she went through when she was young. This is referred to time and again to remind the character (and perhaps the audience as well?) to not get over-weight in order to fit in and dwell on vanity if you want to be the most popular girl in your social circle. At least 27 women respondents variously mentioned "appearances", "looks", "hairstyle", and "clothing style" in their detailed replies to what attracts them to the show.

In the survey I also asked the respondents to construct the image of Manhattan that they form in their mind while watching the show. Some recurring adjectives included "free" and "freedom" along with "love", "open about sexuality", "modern" and "young". While it will not be wrong to suggest that the Manhattan of the show is hardly representative of Manhattan in real life, it will be useful to discuss the lack of any racial and ethnic diversity on the show. There are no Hispanic or Black characters even peripherally present in the show or sexual diversity in terms of characters other than those of the heterosexual kind. There is also a discernible air of anti-intellectualism embedded within the show, where one of the characters who holds a doctorate and is a paleontologist is made fun of, stopped from discussing his work or publications, is branded as boring and is derided as "Not an actual Doctor".[11] None of the other characters ever speak about education, politics or issues plaguing the country or any other subject matter which could be considered "heavy". Any references to the economy are limited to their own personal jobs and the amount of money they make. The show in that sense is largely conformist to idealized notions of good house, good job, and money to spend, with person to love and maintaining the status quo. It is not surprising that the one-page brief for the show was that the show will be about six friends who hang out at the coffee house.[12]

Re-living the show: Online Fan Practices

The field of cultural studies and research on media texts as artefacts of culture has certainly helped transcend the previous assumptions around meaning-making and the ways of seeing and knowing. Much of the research in the field of cultural studies has firmly argued that the meaning of a text is not embedded in the text itself but the meaning is generated when the audience encounters the text and engages with it. While the first level of production of a cultural text may be guided by the dominant mode and logic of culture industry production, it is in fact the second order of production (consumption) by way of which the audience receives, makes use of and interacts with the text (Certeau, 1984). Michel de Certeau calls this active consumption of texts as "poaching" (pp. 74). HenryJenkins (1992) calls this active consumption "textual poaching" and fans as "active cultural producers" and notes the various ways in which fans may engage with a text, including recontextualization (where fans may add to the text's narrative and offer explanations), cross-overs (cross-referencing other television programmes and characters) and personalization (fans inserting themselves in the narrative).

During the course of my survey, it emerged that for the audiences, post-viewing engagement with the show continues to be high with 92% of the respondents agreeing to having read news articles about the show as well as participating in online quizzes themed and centered around the show (76%). Subsequently I carried out online passive participant observation in the group over a period of three months, from May 2020 to July 2020 and kept a track of posts to the group by the members and their interactions with each other over those posts.[13] The group exists as a space of socialization and creative expression, of demonstrating aesthetic and creative labour and continuing the show's narrative by participative community media production. Some of the images circulated in the group are sourced from elsewhere on the Web and some are especially created by the members (more often than not the members mention if the fan art is an original piece of work) The members of the group primarily engaged with each other via the production, circulation and distribution of memes in the group. The members in the group interacted fairly regularly with at least 4 or 5 posts to the group every day. The group's fan practices can be described as sharing of digital texts revolving in and around the show and the content can be categorized in to memes (including still photographs, screenshots and GIFs), quizzes, videos and personal statuses.

Digital memes are the hallmark of our online experience and interaction on the Internet and are a distinctive feature of contemporary popular culture. Memes have existed much before digital communication, when Richard Dawkins in his book *The Selfish Gene*, published in 1976 defined "meme" as a unit of culture, be it a certain kind of behavior or style or even an idea that could spread within a given culture. Dawkins, in conceptualizing the meme, referred to it as a change in culture brought on by mutation on the basis of his theory of selection. The meme as we know now took its current shape and form after it was appropriated by users on the Internet when they drew cultural references from films, cartoons, music videos, video games, photographs etc. to depict an emotion, a phrase or a comment on an issue. The inherent qualities of the Internet meme are its reproduction, reappropriation, and distribution via the Web. It would not be wrong to suggest that the Internet memes we consume now are a meme of Darwin's meme idea itself. The meme then while being an idea, is also a cultural artefact, and in this context, stands at the intersection with fan art production. Shifman (2014, pp 39) suggests a mimetic framework to study memes by "... incorporating several mimetic dimensions... and understanding memes... as groups of content units". While analyzing the memes, it would be useful to look at the form, content, the ideology, stance and the textuality as well as the visuality of the memes.

The immersive fan memes included (i) collage of a scene from the show with the dialogues superimposed in the lower third of the photograph. Often these memes may either be originally created by the group members themselves or saved from other sources from the Web. Often group members also stressed on giving credit to the page or person who originally made the meme, thereby also bringing the idea of authorship to the meme itself, though that is an alien concept to the premise of the meme. Some of these posts have members commenting on that scene from the show with their own interpretation or opinion, some of these comments also involve drawing examples from the member's own personal lives.The other category of memes on the page includes (ii) screenshots or GIFs (Graphic Interchange Format) of a scene that stands as a referent to the episode itself or the specific scene in question. Such posts have members commenting with the dialogues in the said scene or their favorite part of the dialogue from the scene, with other member's reaffirming or suggesting why a character did what they did in the scene.A form of personalized meme category includes (iii) still photographs from the show with the creator's own message superimposed on the photograph. The content of some of these messages varies from 'Why I like this character?' or 'Why I like this couple on the show?'. More often than not the message also includes why they want something similar in their own lives.Another nostalgic memorialization via the meme included (iv) using every character's standard phrases superimposed on their photographs or screenshots. On such posts members usually up vote the phrases they like the best and also the ones they immensely dislike. Members also tag their friends from within the group drawing their attention to the post.Cross-over memes and those referring to other trending phrases or memes on the Web is also popular on the group with (v) juxtaposition of trending memes or phrases on the internet with the characters of the show. This kind of cross-referencing also included juxtaposing a screenshot and a dialogue from the show with another show and dialogue in a kind of cross-textual referencing. In one of the recent posts in July 2020 a lot of cross-textual references between another popular show *Game of Thrones* led to many such memes. Some memes also include (vi) members posting a screenshot from the show and suggesting alternate endings in the episode or an entirely new story and (vii) superimposing the names of the show's characters on stock images taken from the Internet or other popular culture references.

Members also share short video clippings of specific scenes that they like, captioned with their own take on the scene, inviting comments from other users and tagging their friends to take part in the conversation. Such posts lead to fascinating discussions on the member's own version of why a character behaved the way they did or disagreeing with other members on motives, statements and behavior of the characters. Another very popular way of engaging with the show on the group is sharing online quizzes themed around the show with other members of the group. There are perhaps hundreds s of online quizzes about the show available on the Web and on any given day at least one quiz is shared by a member. Among the various kinds of quizzes, members share quizzes about specific characters such as "Do you know him or her?", "Are you more like him or her?", "Which profession from the characters should you have had?" and "How much do you really know the show?" among others. Such posts lead to members posting their scores, sharing trivia about the show with others and posting explanations about the quiz.Members also post personal statuses from in and around the show, such as a long-standing joke from the show, or an unresolved conflict from the show, which they'd like other members to weigh in on. Some personal statuses also take the form of questions where members ask the group who they identify with the most or discuss a contemporary issue and wonder how the characters of the show respond to it. More recently, there have been cross-reference questions such as how a character from this show would have responded to a situation from another show if given a chance. Such posts attract passionate discussions, many disagreements and hypothetical arguments.

The pleasures of watching: Some Notes

The television and OTT culture industry may find reruns profitable, but for the audiences of the show, it remains iconic not just on television but also in their video-on-demand and online streaming choices where they consciously seek out the show. The show certainly obfuscates class conflict, racial inequality and alienation of labour. It squarely puts the onus of survival on the individual, where Monica, a budding chef needs to find her own footing while wading through endless catering jobs and compromises with multinational food corporations. While the show also obliquely refers to struggle, it only does that in passing, where Ross, an emerging scholar and academician negotiates the complex world of tenure and academia. Joey, a struggling actor, has to pull himself together to get regular acting jobs in order to keep his medical insurance (there is no mention of an actor's union or a recognized body that works for their welfare). Or someone like Rachel, who learns that she cannot always be her daddy's spoilt rich kid, but she'll have to be her own spoilt rich kid. Chandler on the other hand is the smart corporate whiz who saves enough for a rainy day, and still has unresolved issues with his father's sexuality and occupation as a drag performer. Phoebe on the other hand is the only character who is allowed to criticize mass production, standardization and commodification only because she is – as one of the characters in the show describes her – 'flaky'. She is unpredictable, weird and eccentric, someone who believes in ghosts, spirits and auras, and hence by extension most of her beliefs are untenable and to be brushed off. My respondents to the survey as well as those interviewed described watching the show as a leisurely activity and discussed the pleasures derived from the show at length. Barring a few – who did mention that the show brings forward the challenges of living in a city like Manhattan – none of the respondents chose to reflect on the socio-political issues underlining the show. For majority of them, the show was just that, situation comedy among six friends.

The undying appeal of the show is exactly this, footloose and fancy free, every man (or woman) for himself (or herself). Though one can rely on friends to bail us out and provide comfort, the state has no role to play, its presence is only a mild irritant, at best. The show is the representation of the best that 'American life' has to offer: freedom, autonomy and choice. The pleasures of watching the show are also inextricably linked with its long-standing popular culture presence on the Web. For the members of the fan group, the show and its characters are seamlessly integrated with their everyday digital practices of sharing jokes, memes and posts on social media, on the group and off it.The show is non-confrontational and equally liked by advertisers. In that sense the fact that the show makes no external reference to social issues, economy or polity, it continues to exist in suspended animation in a timeless space, much like a heterotopia, and perhaps that's the reason it continues to find relevance even 13 years after the last episode was aired. As one of the respondent's put it, *"It is a clean show and touches a chord every time, every human emotion and every conflict a person may go through is in the show"*.

Before writing this paper, I assumed that the show's audiences would lament the unavailability of other situational comedies and similar content produced in India or even similar content from the West. However, it does emerge that there is no dearth of content, with different shows finding their presence and following among the audiences' viewing habits. This particular show however continues to be that familiar space most Indian audiences continue to return to, find relevant, seek comfort in, and identify with their life, not just as banal television but as a meaningful repository of love, relationships and friendship.

Endnotes:

[1]A detailed discussion of the study is available here, http://www.buffalo.edu/news/releases/2012/09/13646.html

[2]For a more in-depth discussion on the Indian television experience post the 1990s within the framework of globalization, refer to Narayan, Sunetra Sen. Globalization and Television: A Study of the Indian Experience, 1990-2010. New Delhi. Oxford University Press. 2013. The book examines in detail the liberalization of the television space, opening up of the economy, rise in purchasing power, developments in telecommunication and the concomitant changes in audiences, channels, available content, revenue models etc.

[3]BARC defines impressions as television viewership in thousands of a target audience who viewed a show, averaged across minutes, for more see, http://www.barcindia.co.in/glossary-terms.aspx

[4]For instance, this report from 2016 on a reunion http://www.cnbc.com/2016/01/14/friends-cast-to-be-reunited.html

[5]Report on the earnings and loyalty figures of the cast, https://www.usatoday.com/story/life/entertainthis/2015/02/27/youll-never-believe-how-much-money-the-friends-cast-still-earns-today/77593556/, viewed on 1st May, 2017

[6]Report on the loyalty and syndication rights deal, http://www.nytimes.com/2002/02/12/business/friends-deal-will-pay-each-of-its-6-stars-22-million.html, viewed on 1st May, 2017

[7]Figures on the revenue model and DVD sales figures, http://money.cnn.com/2004/04/27/news/fortune500/friends_dvd/, viewed on 1st May, 2017

[8]Report on Romedy Now's assessment of the show, http://www.indiantelevision.com/television/tv-channels/english-entertainment/romedy-now-banks-on-popular-90s-sitcom-friends-140619, viewed on 15th May 2017. Binge-watching is a relatively new term with reference to television shows first experienced due to easy availability of television episodes online via OTT platforms. Rather that watching one episode per day or week (depending on the scheduling) on TV, audiences can also choose to watch more than one episode in one sitting online. This has also led television networks to run back-to-back episodes, especially on the weekends to hold on to audience share.

[9]A comparative report on online streaming statistics of two popular shows, http://www.vogue.com/article/seinfeld-vs-friends-streaming, viewed on 16th May 2017

[10]This article also discusses other transmedia activities around the show such as portals like Buzzfeed.com doing regular features and short stories on the show and its characters or quizzes

[11]For instance, in Season 10, episode thirteenth, Ross and Rachel are in the hospital where Rachel tells him not to call himself a doctor (with a PhD) since the word doctor means something in the hospital.

[12]The article on the continued fan following of the show can be accessed here, http://www.dailymail.co.uk/home/you/article-2465332/Friends-Why-loving-hit-TV-20-years-on.html, viewed on 20th May, 2017

[13]The field site for the study was a closed Facebook fan group based on the show. Passive participant observation involved accessing the group daily and maintaining field notes of activities of the members including comments and posts

References

1. Appadurai, A. (1990). "Disjuncture and Difference in the Global Cultural Economy". *Theory Culture Society* 7: 295-310

2. Battles, K. and Hilton-Morrow, W. (2002). "Gay Characters in Conventional Spaces: Will and Grace and the Situation Comedy Genre."*Critical Studies in Media Communication* 19 (1): 87-105

3. Chopra, R. and Gajjala, R. (2012). *Global Media, Culture and Identity: Theory, Cases and Approaches*. New York: Routledge.

4. Certeau, M. (1984). *The Practice of Everyday Life.* California: University of California.

5. Dawkins, R. (1976). *The Selfish Gene.* Oxford: Oxford University Press.

6. Hall, S. (1997). The Local and the Global: Globalization and Ethnicity' in Anthony D. King (eds) *Culture, Globalization and the World-System: Contemporary Conditions for the Representation of Identity.* Minnesota, University of Minnesota Press.

7. Hill, A. (2007). *Restyling Factual Television: Audiences and news, documentary and reality genres.* New York: Routledge.

8. Horton, A (2019, October 8). The last laugh: behind the multimillion-dollar deals to buy old sitcoms. *The Guardian.* https://www.theguardian.com/tv-and-radio/2019/oct/08/the-last-laugh-behind-the-multimillion-dollar-deals-to-buy-old-sitcoms

9. Jenkins, H. (1992). *Textual Poachers: Television Fans and Participatory Culture.* New York: Routledge.

10. Kompare, D. (2005). *Rerun Nation: How Repeats Invented American Television.* Routledge.

11. McGonigal, K (2012, Semtember 11). Watching Your Favorite TV Show Can Boost Your Willpower. *Psychology Today.* https://www.psychologytoday.com/blog/the-science-willpower/201209/watching-your-favorite-tv-show-can-boost-your-willpower, viewed on 15th May 2017

12. Morley, D. (1986). *Family Television: Cultural Power and Domestic Leisure.* London: Routledge.

13. Sathe, G. (2012). 'What India Watched: 2012 Youtube Rewind.' *The Live Mint,* December 18 . http://www.livemint.com/Leisure/TqPt0GUTdJ5Mj6nbMicDdJ/What-India-watched-2012-YouTube-rewind.html(viewed on 30th May, 2017)

14. Shifman, L. (2014). *Memes in Digital Culture.* Massachusetts: Massachusetts Institute of Technology.

15. Spigel, L. (1995). "From the Dark ages to the golden age: women's memories and television reruns"*Screen,* 36 (1): 16–33.

16. Sternbergh, A. (2016). "Is 'Friends' Still the Most Popular Show on TV?" The Vulture.March 20. http://www.vulture.com/2016/03/20-somethings-streaming-friends-c-v-r.html (accessed on 1st May 2017)

CHAPTER VII

A study on Japanese Anime series in India: with special reference to Tamil dubbed series

M.Viji, Dept. of Journalism & Communication, University of Madras, Chepauk, Chennai,Tamilnadu.

Abstract:

Children in India are exposed to a variety of content, from cartoon shows to educational programs, on more than 17 cartoon channels that are available in both English and regional languages. It all began with Cartoon Network, India's first 24-hour cartoon channel. Now Nick, Hungama, Disney, Pogo, etc are there in India especially for children audience. In these channels, some animated series are quite popular among Indian children. According to various sources, Tom and Jerry, Pokemon, Doraemon, Ninja hattori, Chhota bheem, Shin-chan, Mr.Bean, Oggy and cockroaches, Hagemaru and Motupatlu are the most viewed animated series in India. Among these top 10 series, five anime series are imported from the country Japan. Japanese manga anime series are popular all over the world. Manga,the comic books arepopular in Japan. As a result, Manga has become well-known among fans of animation everywhere.The Pokémon anime had a 100.8 million-viewer audience in India in 2014. This study aims to identify the Japanese series which are dubbed in Tamil, the reasons for its attractions among children, what are the elements do the children like in Japanese anime series,etc. To get answers for these questions, this study will adopt Focus group discussion method. 15 children from two districts from Tamil Nadu, participates in this discussion.

Keywords: Anime, Children, focus group discussion, television.

Introduction

Children of Millennials and Generation Z raised up by watching Japanese animated television series like Pokémon, Beyblade, Dragan Ball Z, Doreamon and many others without even realizing it that these are Japanese series. Any type of animation from any country is referred to as "anime" in Japanese.Anime, every so often known as Japanimation, is an immensely popular type of illustrated media from Japan(Japanyugen - Everything You Wondered About Japan, 2020).Japanese "anime" is one of the most famous forms of animation. It is a phenomenon of contemporary popular culture (Napier,2001).Its reach among children all over the world is huge. Japan produces more than 60% of the world's animated tv programs(*JapanYugen - Everything You Wondered About Japan*, 2020).It has its own unique style of stories, character's physical features, colorful graphics, ninja (a spy or assassin with old Japanese martial arts training, notably in the past(merriam-webster.com). It has been very popular in India and influenced Indian children enormously. Doreamon and Shinchan almost reached every Indian houses. This study is about the Japanese anime which are dubbed in Tamil language. So, first we see the history and development of Japanese anime and its reach in India.

History and Development of Animation in Japan:

Oten Shimokawa started working on creating animation, and his debut movie, Mukuzo Imokawa, the Concierge, had its premiere in January 1917. The following year, Seitaro Kitayama established the first Japanese animation company. Kitayama Eiga Seisakujo (Kitayama Movie Factory), but he vanished soon after the Great Kanto earthquake of 1923, which caused extensive damage. The Great Kanto earthquake that levelled Tokyo obliterated every print of early Japanese animation. When the animation industry initially began to emerge shortly after, Sanae Yamamoto, Yasuji Murata, and Noburo Ofuji—three prolific and significant early animators from Japan who began their careers in the late 1920s—were among those who were exposed to the world. Murata invented the usage of cel animation after studying western animation techniques. Ofuji concentrated on making drawings out of cut paper and also played around with sound and colour.

The first Japanese animated film with sound was Whale, while the first with an authentic recorded soundtrack was Black Kitty (1931). The Japanese military's invasion of Manchuria at the beginning of the 1930s sparked a rise in nationalism and changed the usual subject of early Japanese animations from folk stories to anti-Western domestic propaganda, like the Black Cat Hooray! Takao Nakano (April 1934). After a relatively calm era between 1934 and 1937, Japan declared war on China in July 1937. The majority of the animations made after that were therefore nationalistic movies. Japan animations were mostly used for internal military propaganda when World War II ended in 1939. The Japanese Imperial Navy provided full assistance, including finance, limited production supplies, and even released animators from the requirement to serve in the military. The Spider and the Tulip (1943), directed by Kenzo

Masaoka, is a well-known example of this era's animated films. The Spider and the Tulip, which included actual flowers as well as a cartoon spider and ladybird, is still regarded by some reviewers as Japan's best animated movie.

Ozamu Tezuka, referred to as "the Disney of Japan" and "the God of Comic (Manga no Kamisama)," is one of the key figures in the development and history of Japanese animation.In 1962, he entered the world of animation by founding Mushi Production after introducing cinematic art direction to the Japanese comic industry. Throughout the 1960s, it developed into a significant animation company, producing animated films including Kimba the White Lion and Astro Boy. Later, both of these animations were aired in syndication in the US. Additionally, he promoted the idea that animation is not just for kids by creating cartoons with unusual themes like Legend of the Forest and leaping, as well as other works with an emphasis on humanity.The 1980s saw a continuation of the fresh direction Tezuka gave Japanese animation.

Direct to video productions, often known as original video animations (OVAs), have begun to appear alongside the more conventional television and film feature animations. The themes depicted in the animations are also growing more varied and diverse, covering anything from humour to adult themes to huge robots. These themes are usually based on World War II events. Together with Isao Takahata, Hayao Miyazaki founded Studio Ghibli, which went on to become the next great name in Japanese animation. His 2001 animated film Spirited Away went on to win an Academy Award in 2002.Although there were strong criticisms that Japanese animation had gone artistically bankrupt with no new concepts being generated, the 1990s saw the growth of Japanese animation into a global phenomenon. The Pokemon phenomenon, which originated as a video game before exploding into TV shows and a number of animated films, likewise began in the 1990s.Japanese animation has not only embraced the development of digital technology at the start of the twenty-first century, but it has also established itself as a key player in the animation sector. The Animatrix (2002), an anthology of various animated films based on the film Matrix, was one of them. It was directed primarily by Japanese filmmakers and produced by the Japanese animation studios.

Japanese Animation in India

As Japan's culture has an impact on India, Indians are generally growing more interested in it.Japanese anime has increased significantly more quickly than other television genres in children's television programming in India. Animax India used to stream solely anime, 24 hours a day. The channel continued to air young adult-oriented anime for adult viewers and used to stream anime on the same day as Japan. Later, Animax India stopped airing programmes in India. A variety of other stations, including Disney Channel, Sonic, Nickelodeon, Hungama TV, and Super Hungama (previously Disney XD, Jetix, and Marvel HQ), also air anime at various times.Additionally, anime is accessible via the YouTube channels for Muse Asia, Muse India, and Ani-One Asia, as well as on Netflix, Crunchyroll, Amazon Prime Video, Disney+ Hotstar, bilibili, NHK World-Japan, Voot Kids, and Tubi (Wikipedia.org). Initially through animax channelas, anime was aired to 15-25 years old audience. Later, Toonami and Cartoon Network were both owned by Turner International India. Turner International India debuted a distinct channel called Toonami in 2015. It broadcast animated series including Dragon Ball Z and Inzauma Eleven.After that, lots of anime series dubbed and aired in India and it became the popular series among Indians. When Japanese anime entered the world of culture and entertainment in the 1990s, the growth of "otakus" and "weebs" in India began.The public was more receptive to the inflow of anime as a result of anime like Doraemon and Shinchan breaking into the Indian market (Shroff, 2022).

Review of Literature:

The study, "A new perspective on the first Japanese animation" discusses the earliest Japanese animation film, its pioneers, the significance of Tezuka, as well as the origin, style, and form of Japanese animation.

Ruchi Jaggi examined the content of Japanese cartoon which are telecasting in Indian children's television channels by tracing its progression from 2000 to 2012.In order to put the ubiquity and appeal of imported content on Indian children's television channels in context, she also examined academic studies on children's television in India. She mentioned the annual revenue and its growth in television medium in india, the reach of television medium in india, especially among india children. When mentioning about the interviews in here reviews, she told that childrenexpressed admiration for all the foreign-produced animated television series they watched, claiming that they were more creative and enjoyable.She also has tried a couple of limited scope studies on the popularity of Japanese animation shows on Indian children's television channels, and she found that the "Japanese wave" is omnipresent on children's television in India. She mentioned Challapalli's words here about

Japanese cartoons in Indian television in detail that, even with a quick glance at the programme schedules, it is very clear that there are many Japanese cartoons can be found on Indian children's television networks. Local television networks like Hungama, which started airing Japanese animation in 2004, were able to overtake market leaders Cartoon Network and Pogo within a period of two to three years because to the popularity of Japanese shows. Following the popularity of Hungama, all the other networks started to buy and air Japanese cartoon programmes.Ninja Hattori, the most well-liked Japanese anime, is one of the channel drivers for Nick India, even though Hungama has the highest percentage of Japanese programming. The popularity of Ninja Hattori, coupled with the non-Japanese Dora the Explorer, Ninja Hattori, and Oggy and the Cockroaches, which reach audiences in Hindi, Tamil, and Telugu in addition to English, was noted by Nina Elavia Jaipuria, Senior Vice President & General Manager, Nick India. TAM Media claims that these programmes have given the channel the largest share of the Hindi-speaking markets (24% among 4–14 years old in July 2010).

The book Japanese Animation in Asia gives a thorough analysis of the technological advancements, industrial structure, historical evolution, and globalization dynamics of Japanese animation. The production logics of anime, its characteristics as an "emotion industry," and the contribution of many Asian nations to the creation, consumption, and cultural influence of Japanese animation are all covered in specific chapters. In the second part of the book a study is there regarding response to anime &manga in Indian context. There he said about the reach of Doreamon and Shin chan among Indian children. The author mentioned Pillalamarri's words about Indian audience for Japanese cartoons as, similar varied reactions have been shown by the Indian community at large to the reception practices of the Indian admirers of Japanese pop culture. On the one hand, these fans are praised for their fandom pursuits since they are thought to be cool and trendy and help to strengthen the bonds between India and Japan.When he interviewed Indian fans of Japaense cartoons, he found that, with the help of Japanese popular culture texts, Indian lovers can escape the monotony and tension of their everyday life. They are inspired and motivated by anime and manga, which also helps them feel better when they're having a bad day. According to a participant in the interview, "When I watch anime, then I don't think about anybody else." I simply exist in my own world, the author stated.

A variety of perspectives from media professionals, designers, teachers, and academics from in the East Asian Pacific are included in the book Japanese Animation: East Asian Perspectives. This collection not only uses a multidisciplinary approach to comprehend the topic of Japanese animation, but it also demonstrates how to do research, impart knowledge, and more thoroughly investigate this multifaceted world. This volume offers a rare but crucial perspective on how mutual influences of animation thrive among East Asian cultures and the types of transnational exchange they foster, in contrast to many English-language books on Japanese animation that concentrate on how Western cultures are influenced by Japanese popular culture.

The article 'Disney to Doreamon' by Ruchi Jaggi concluded that Two problems were specifically related to children's television in India: the imbalance between supply and demand, as well as the lack of a global market for locally produced Indian animation programs that are heavily based on mythology and folklore and so had a tendency to become repetitive. This discrepancy between supply and demand was filled by the broadcast of Japanese animation on Indian television. The main characters, themes, and narratives of anime are suitable for children to understand. These were a departure from the conventional mythological and folk tales as well as from the American television programs, which provided a backdrop that was quite repetitive. Hindi and other regional languages were dubbed skillfully, and it was successful.Because of the success of these shows, newcomers like Hungama have been able to overtake established competitors like Cartoon Network and Pogo in the top spots within a period of two to three years. Due to the popularity of this trend, all other networks have been inspired to buy and air Japanese animation programmes. Nick (the highest rated channel) airs the most well-known Japanese anime, Ninja Hattori, which is in fact one of the channel drivers for Nick India even though Hungama has the highest percentage of Japanese programming.

Cresswell examined the disparities between modern western animation and contemporary eastern animation as well as the preconceived beliefs surrounding both. He investigated this by conducting case studies of well-known figures who have advanced the medium in some way, concentrating on how they have transcended their own countries to become icons on the stage of global culture.While explaining about cross-pollination of western and eastern culture of animation. The immensely popular Pokémon media property, created in Japan in 1996 and introduced to the west in 1997, is a more contemporary example of how cartoons have interacted. The franchise's success in both the east and west suggests that it is more relatable and current on a human level than on a regional level. The franchise's unmistakable leader and "the most adored cartoon character since Hello Kitty" is Pikachu. (1999, Time Magazine). The idea for Pikachu was similar to that of Hello Kitty in that it was loosely based on an animal, in this case a mouse, and given a simple design with a primary colour. Yellow was chosen as the primary colour because it is easily recognisable by children and is gender neutral, and special consideration was given to the fact that Winnie the Pooh was the only other primary yellow mascot at the time (Cresswell, 2015).

After reviewing the books and articles regarding the researcher found that there are no studies on Japanese cartoons which are dubbed in Tamil language and no studies are therefrom the perspective of children. So, this study aimed to get the children's view about Japanese anime. Focus Group method is used here to find their view and likes and dislikes on cartoon series with particle to Japanese anime series.

Research Method:

This study has done under focus group method. Focus group method gives perceptions into human thought processes and a deeper comprehension of the things being examined. So, unlike survey which mostly uses closed ended questions or unlike interviews to get in-depth information which is not possible all the time due to its expenses and lack of resources, the focus group method gives the researchermore detailed information more affordably than in-depth interviews.In this study, the researcher would like to get the information about the Japanese animation from the children's standpoint. So, the researcher adopted focus group method.

Sampling:

There are two sampling required for this study. Both the samples are selected under purposive sampling.

1. Samples of Japanese Anime series
2. Samples of Participants for the focus group discussion

Sample for Japanese Anime series:

This study selected the Japanese Anime series which are telecasted in India, with particular to the series which are dubbed in Tamil language.

Japanese Anime are available in Television, particular websites, YouTube and OTT platforms. This study will take the series which are running in Indian television channels only. Cartoon Network, Sonic, Nickelodeon, Hungama TV, Disney Channel and Super Hungama (formerly Disney XD, Jetix and Marvel HQ) are the channels which broadcast anime series.There have been 40 anime series in Cartoon network, 20 in Pogo, 15 in Toonami, 7 in Nickelodeon, 14 in Nickelodeon Sonic, 14 in Disney XD, 33 in Hungama,9 in Disney, 5 insuper Hungama (marvel hq), 1 inDisney international HD, 1 in Sony yay and 3 in Zeecafe. From this population the anime series which are in air now and dubbed in tamil language have been taken as sample for discussion. Accordingly, it's been shortlisted to Doraemon, Shinchan, Perman, Pokemon, Ninja hattori, Hagemaru, kiteretsu Daihyakka andNaruto.

Samples for Participants for the focus group discussion:

The researcher, here, taken sample of 15 children in the age of 12 years old. Two groups of children were formed. One group is from Chennai district, another group is from Chengalpattu district (which is next to Chennai) from Tamil Nadu. So, one group is from urban area and another group is from rural area. Both of these children are studying in Private schools.

The reason to select twelve years old children is, these children have been watching cartoons almost a decade. They have been introduced to various types of television cartoons, Websites &YouTube and OTT platforms. Added, the stages of a child's cognitive development are described by Piaget. According to him intelligence progresses through various phases as it develops. Instead, there are distinctions between the thinking of early children and older children on both a qualitative and quantitative level.

The four stages of cognitive development, Piaget says:

Birth through two years is the sensorimotor stage.

Pre operation stage: 2 to 7.

Ages 7 to 11 are the specific operational stage.

Ages 12 and older for the formal operating stage.

Children start to develop their ability to think abstractly at the age of 11 or 12. They end the "concrete operational time," as Piaget called it, and move into the "formal operational period." Children learn to employ deductive reasoning during formal operations, which means they can be taught a general principle and apply it to a particular scenario. Children who participate in formal operations can develop plans, think like scientists, and rigorously test answers (Cognitive Development in 11-13 Yearsold/Scholastic/Parents, n.d.). So,if the study/discussion made with the children in formal operating stage, it will be fruitful. These children obviously know the difference between reality and imaginary, culture between countries, they have logical and scientific skills. To study about the anime series these age groups are pertinent.

Findings and Analysis:

Discussion with Chennai children happened after school hours at the park area of one of the children's house society and discussion with the Chengalpattu children happened after school hours only, but in school campus, as the children come from different locations, so,it's not possible to assemble them in one area.

But there are lots of similarities betweenthese two groupson children's media habits and their favorite television programs and cartoon series.These children watch cartoons almost from their toddler stage.

The participants discussed the following:

1. The cartoon shows/programs they watch from their toddler stage (if any).
2. Type of cartoons they watch at the current stage.
3. Their favorite cartoon programsseries andhow long they watch those.
4. The language they used to watch cartoon series.
5. The medium they watch cartoons.
6. The origin or the original language of the cartoon series they watch.
7. Type of Japanese series they like to watch andthe reasons for preference of watching Japanese anime series.
8. The aspects of Japanese animation they enjoy the most.
9. With whom they watch cartoon shows?
10. Do their parents allow them to watch cartoon series?

The findings of the discussion follows:

1. These children used to watch Dora the explorer, Ben 10, Thomas, Chotta bheem, Doreamon, Jackie Chan adventures, Tom & Jerry, Phineas &Ferb, Peppa pig,Mighty Raju, Fukerey boyzz and Grizzy & the lemmings in their childhood,i.e., till their 5th standard.

2. Currently, they often watch Ben10, Doraemon, Naruto, Shinchan, Pokemon, Selfie with Bajrangi, Attack on Titan, Hagemaru, Dragon Ballz, Teen titans,Grizzy and the lemmings andNinja Hattori.

3. All the kids from these groups like to watch Japanese cartoons namely Doraemon, Pokemon, Shinchan and Naruto.

4. They used to watch these series in television. Three children watch Naruto in a website, as they don't have tv at home.

5. Some children watch Pokémon in OTT platforms for repetition.

6. Most of the children watch these series in Tamil dubbed version and some in English if not available in Tamil language.

7. Half of the children know the origin of the cartoon they watch and know that those are Japanese series.

8. They prefer actionseries, for example Ninja fights and fights with unique animals (example; Bulbasaur, Charmander, Pikachu)

9. They like to watch cartoon series because of elements such as comical dialogues, action sequences, plots, gadgets, the unique physique and characters.

10. Children used to watch these series with their siblings. Most of the parents don't say anything for watching these series. Few parents oppose to watch Shinchan due to dialogues.

Analysis:

The participants of this study share their views and perceptions enthusiastically, look as if this is their favorite subject. Through the discussion, the researcher found thatthe children love to watch cartoon series andthey prefer Japanese anime series. By their childhood they watched all kind of cartoon series, viz., Indian, American and Japanese. However,when they grow, theypick Japanese series and few children select both American and Japanese series.Due to the covid-19 pandemic, kids started watching series in Ott platforms too. Three, out of these 15 children don't have television at home,hence they watch Naruto series in a website.

Children watch their favorite cartoon everyday a minimum of one hour. In the weekend they watch at least three hours. Doraemon movies, Pokémon movies or Naruto episodes are their weekend preferences.During the discussion they often speak about the characters in Doraemon, Shinchan and Pokemon. The gadgets of doraemon and the funny dialogues of Shinchan, the action scenes of Pokemons are their favorites. They argue with each other thatseries which have the best fight sceneswhether Naruto or Pokemon. Most of them prefer Pokemons. Due to the different, yet understandable plots and unique featured animals are the attractive elements in Pokemon. Comparatively, boys watch cartoon series more than girls. Girls prefer to watch videos in Youtube. While discussion, the observer found that boys prefer Pokemon and girls prefer Doraemon and Shinchan.

Conclusion:

Though people of India are not aware of the country Japan or its culture much, they are familiar with Japanese cartoon characters. The year 1989, The jungle book - tv series aired in was a Japanese Anime. People watched it without knowing the country which made the series. The same is happening now. Without even comprehending it, Millennials and Generation Z grew up watching Japanese animated television series like Pokémon, Doraemon, Shinchan and many others. The reason behind this is the elements in Japanese series are enthralling the audience. Unique plots and characterization, simple and humorous dialogues, imaginative scenes entertain the children than any other programs. The stereotypical stories and characters of Indian and American animation make it monotonous and make the children to prefer Japanese series which are interesting to watch.Merchandization also plays major role here. The researcher found that, kids aware of the series through the products like Pokemon Trading card (Over 43.2 billion Pokemon cards have been sold globally (bing.com), Doraemon dolls, bags, etc stimulate the children to seek and watch the anime series.

Recommendations for future study:

Future studies can be done in the Content of Japanese series, the impact of Japanese series in the Indian animation industry, the influence of dubbing in regional languages.

References:

1. Cognitive Development in 11-13 Year Olds | Scholastic | Parents. (n.d.). Cognitive Development in 11-13 Year Olds | Scholastic | Parents. Retrieved September 20, 2022, from https://www.scholastic.com/

2. Cresswell, J. (n.d.). Cross-Pollination of Animation: Western Cartoons & Japanese Animation - Academia.Edu. Retrieved September 21, 2022, fromhttps://www.academia.edu/25524158/

3. Drazen, P. (2002). Anime Explosion! In The What? Why? and Wow! of Japanese Animation. https://doi.org/10.1604/9781880656723

4. Jaggi, R. (2014). An Overview of Japanese Content on Children's Television in India. Media Asia, 41(3), 240–254. https://doi.org/10.1080/01296612.2014.11690021

5. Jaggi, R. (2011). From Disney to Doraemon - Japanese Anime substitute American Animation on Indian Children's Television: A trend study. Amity Journal of Media and Communication Studies, Vol. 1, Number 1, ISSN 2231-1033.

6. Japan Yugen - Everything You Wondered About Japan. (2020, November 6). Japan Yugen. japanyugen.com

7. Lopez, A.(2012). A new perspective on the first Japanese animation. ISBN:978-989-97567-6-2.

8. Napier, S. (2001). Anime from Akira to Princess Mononoke. In Experiencing Contemporary Japanese Animation. https://doi.org/10.1604/9780312299408

9. Pellitteri, M., & Heung-Wah, W. (2021). Japanese Animation in Asia. In Transnational Industry, Audiences, and Success. Routledge. https://doi.org/10.4324/9781315123707

10. Shroff, D. (2022, June 13). Influence Of Japanese Anime in India. ED Times | Youth Media Channel. https://edtimes.in/

Representation of Women in Turkish Drama Series Popular in India: A Content Analysis

Sanchita Mehrotra, Ph.D. Scholar, Amity School of Communication, Amity University, Lucknow Campus,Uttar Pradesh

Dr. Rashmi Kumari, Assistant Professor, Department of Mass Communication, Karim City College, Jamshedpur, Jharkhand

Abstract

The real influence of television drama is reaching heterogeneous population with fundamental source of awareness, information, education and importantly entertainment. It impacts the thought process of viewers. The Information and Communication Technologies facilitate to cross the territories. Audience are benefitting as within a click they may access the favorite dramas, programs, cinemas and news of any country according to their time preference. From last decade the popularity of Turkish dramas has flourished in India. OTT platforms, Channels Apps are providing Turkish dramas in Hindi and Urdu dubbed with English subtitles. The woman has been regarded as secondary to the man in the existing society, therefore they have to fight for their image, identity and existence. The aim of the study is to analyze the representation of women character inTurkish Drama series popular in India by employing content analysis. The Girl Named Feriha and Fatmagul are the two popular Turkish drama series selected for this study. This paper will utilize Bell Hook's Feminist theory of oppression. It will thus, examine that how women are represented in Turkish drama series and reveal the status of women portrayed at global platform.

Keywords: Turkish Drama, Women, Representation, Feminism

Introduction

The real influence of television drama is reaching heterogeneous population with fundamental source of awareness, information, education and importantly entertainment. It impacts the thought process of viewers. The Information and Communication Technologies facilitate to cross the territories. Audience are benefitting as within a click they may access the favorite dramas, programs, cinemas and news of any country according to their time preference. From last decade the popularity of Turkish dramas has flourished in India. OTT platforms, Channels Apps are providing Turkish dramas in Hindi and Urdu dubbed with English subtitles. The woman has been regarded as secondary to the man in the existing society, therefore they have to fight for their image, identity and existence.

Bell Hooks' Feminist Theory

Bell hooks' known as Feminist Theory Revolutionary and started writing her own feminist theory in 1984. During that time various feminists have been debating about the definition of feminism and what it meant to be part of the feminist movement. There was a question of what feminists fought for and ought to fight for. Contrasting interpretations of feminist theory sprung left and right, paving the way for a new brand of confusion in the movement (hooks 2000,6). Misconceptions were prevalent, particularly, that feminism is all about women wanting to become men. Making this problem the core of her earlier writings, hooks stated that without a well-grounded definition, feminism will lose what it stood for. She writes:

(The) central problem within feminist discourse has been our inability to either arrive at a consensus of opinion about what feminism is or accept definition(s) that could serve as points of unification. Without agreed upon definition(s), we lack a sound foundation on which to construct theory or engage in overall meaningful praxis (hooks 1984, 17).

Without a unifying definition, Hooks feared that feminist politics would be ignored altogether and disinterest in feminism would continue or grow. At this point, she made it her main aim to define feminism, which eventually would pave the way for a more relevant **Revolutionary Feminism.**

In the 1980s, feminism, then also known as "women's lib", was simply known in popular culture (although not among feminist scholars) as the movement fighting for equal rights between men and women. This was problematic on that level, since it gave rise to the following questions such as: "which men do women want to be equal to?" and "do women share a common vision of what equality means?" (hooks 1984, 18). She wanted to develop a definition of feminism that was all-encompassing, without neglecting the "other" members of society. Being a black woman living in a white man's world, feminism went beyond the plight of those oppressed by their sexualities. Diversity in terms of race, ethnicity, gender, and many other factors also play vital roles in the exploitation or discrimination of individuals. Writing on the more well-known definition of feminism as the fight for equality between men and women, hooks states,

...implicit in this simplistic definition of women's liberation is a dismissal of race and class as factors that, in conjunction with sexism, determine the extent to which an individual will be discriminated against, exploited or oppressed 1984, 18).

Feminism should include more than just the plight of white Bourgeois women; it should include all those who are exploited, discriminated and/or oppressed.

Feminism started off as a movement to end sexist oppression, but it would be better defined as "the movement to end sexism, sexist exploitation, and oppression" (hooks 2000, viii). This definition "...clearly states that the movement is not about being anti-male. It makes clear that the problem is sexism. And that clarity helps us remember that all of us, female and male, have been socialized from birth on to accept sexist thought and action" (hooks 2000, viii).

Furthermore, this definition makes it clear that if there are oppressed people, there are oppressors as well. Considerably, "females can be just as sexist as men. And while that does not excuse or justify male domination, it does mean that it would be wrong-minded for feminist thinkers to see the movement as simplistically being for women against men" (hooks 2000, ix).

Feminist theory must be revamped to include more than just the plight of privileged women. Marginalized women, or women of other races or classes should make use of their "special vantage points" and take a look at "the dominant racist, classist, sexist hegemony as well as to envision and create a counter-hegemony" (hooks 1984, 15). The participation in this brand of feminist theory is everyone's responsibility. As hooks' book title suggests, Feminism is for everybody (2000).

Revolutionary feminism can make a difference. Through a necessary struggle and a fostering of a critical political consciousness, change is possible.

Interlocking Webs of Oppression

The topic of women's oppression or oppression in general, has been debated on not only by feminist theorists but by philosophers as well. For example, feminist philosopher, Marilyn Frye defines "oppression" and looks at it by extracting the root of the word, which is "press". When one is "oppressed", one is "caught between or among forces and barriers which are so related to each other that jointly they restrain, restrict, or prevent the thing's motion or mobility" (Frye 1998, 46). To further illustrate the definition of oppression, Frye describes the experience of oppressed people:

...the living of one's life is confined and shaped by forces and barriers which are not accidental or occasional and hence avoidable but are systematically related to each other in such a way as to catch one between and among them and restrict or penalize motion in any direction. It is the experience of being caged in: all avenues, in every direction, are blocked or booby-trapped (1998, 46).

To oppress a person is to render this person unable to make his or her own choices. According to hooks, "being oppressed means the absence of choices. It is the primary point of contact between the oppressed and the oppressor" (1984, 5). All throughout modern feminist thought, it has been claimed that, "all women are oppressed". Allegedly, women all throughout the world share a common oppression by virtue of their inherited sex. On the other hand, the diversity of their classes and/or races ends the commonality. While the second wave, Bourgeois white women fight against sexist oppression--racist oppression and classism were generally ignored. Class, race, religion or sexual preference are not given that much importance in the study of women's oppression (hooks 1984, 5).

She admits that sexism is the oldest form of oppression. Feminism, however, must not stop at trying to eradicate sexist oppression per se, as many other forms of oppression stem from sexist oppression. An example would be racist oppression. "Racism as well as class structure is perceived as stemming from sexism. Implicit in this line of analysis is the assumption that the eradication of sexism, the oldest oppression, is necessary before attention can be focused on racism or classism" (hooks 1984, 35). On the other hand, if one focuses too much on only one form of oppression such as sexist or racist, this would be a contradiction.

No one form of oppression deserves more attention than the other. Oppressions are multilayered and they are embodied by sexism, racism, class elitism and imperialism. Consequently, all these are interrelated and inseparably connected to each other. The assumption that these factors can be separated from each other or that they have no impact on each other is wrongheaded and leads to "distorted, biased, and inaccurate" discussions on sexism and sexist oppression (hooks 1981, 12).

Rationale of the study

Nowadays, the dominant theme of serials is anchored on the patriarchal established society. Feminist theory helps us better understand and address unequal and oppressive gender relations. The goal of feminist history is to explore and illuminate the female viewpoint of history through rediscovery of female writers, artists, philosophers, etc., in order to recover and demonstrate the significance of women's voices and choices in the past and present. The representation of women in serial of cross boarders can be perfectly analyzed by **Bell Hooks' Feminist Theory.**

Research Objectives

- The aim of the study is to analyze the representation of women character in Turkish Drama series popular in India by employing content analysis.

Research Questions

- How women are represented in Turkish drama series and reveal the status of women portrayed at global platform?

Research Methodology

The Girl Named Feriha and Fatmagul are the two popular Turkish drama series selected for this study. This paper will utilize Bell Hook's Feminist theory of oppression. The selection of both drama series is selected using purposive sampling because they are popular serials which got telecasted in India at Zee Zindagi television channel in 2013 and are now watchable as series online at MX Player OTT platform as free content.

Analysis and Findings

The two drama series Feriha and Fatmagul episodes were selected as per the methodology framed by the researchers. Season one of both the drama series were watched thoroughly by the researchers to understand the main plot of the dramas and the character sketch of the main characters. Basis on the in-depth study of the two drama series, the researchers identified three main themes for content analysis as:

1.) Women personalities in main role,
2.) Representation of women characters, and
3.) Margin to Central.

The detailed analysis and their findings are discussed as follows:-

Plot Description and story narration in brief:

1. The Girl Named Feriha

Feriha (Hazal Kaya) is a clever and beautiful young girl who lives in a luxury neighbourhood but belongs to a poor family. Her father

(MetinCekmez) works as a maintenance guy in a big apartment block where the management provides them a small living place, at the grand floor of the building.

Feriha's mother (VahideGordum) also helps her father through working as a cleaning lady in the same block. Feriha lives with her parents and her twin brother and sometimes helps her parents to do apartment chores. She collects the trashes, cleans the apartment stairs and carries out the orders of the residents.

Feriha is the only hope of her family. She gets accepted into a private university with a scholarship and immediately gets all the attention of most popular students. At university, everyone thinks that Feriha belongs to a rich family because she looks rich from outside: she wears her rich neighbors clothes and lives in a luxury neighborhood.

However, one day, Fehira's father comes to the university to visit her daughter and at that time, Feriha tells a lie to her friend. She gets embarrassed of her poor father appearing at the university and that's why she says that her father has sent that poor man, a maintenance guy, to the university and that's why she says that her father has sent that poor man, a maintenance guy, to the university to give her something. This one lie turns everything upside down. One lie causes another lie and many others.

This lie also affects Feriha's relationship with Emir (CagatayUlusoy) who is a cool, handsome and rich playboy. They fall in Love each other at first sight but Feriha never discloses that she is a daughter of a poor family.

In the girl named Feriha (adiniferihaKoydum – I named her feriha) TV series story, you will explore a difficult love of Feriha and Emir who are made for each other, yet from different worlds. Also, you will see the struggle of a poor girl among rich people. How long will Feriha be able to continue pretending to be rich? Will Emir discover the truth about Feriha? How will Emir react when he learns all the lies of his first love, Feriha? Will the love of Feriha and Emir stand for all the lies and twists?

1. Fatmagul

Fatmagul is a beautiful and naïve girl who engaged to her childhood sweetheart Mustafa. One night, four young men start to play around with her. They never think that the joke will turn into a rape at first. But later, they begin to rape her, one by one. The sun of her life is shadowed after thar night; it's not only Fatmagul's body which was raped, but also her life.

Mustafa breaks off their engagement and in order to save the honor of her family she is forced to marry one of the rapists, Kerim.

Fatmagul (BerenSaat) is a beautiful and naïve girl who lives Cesme (a touristic place in western Turkey). Due to the death of her parents, she lives with her brother. She plans to get married Mustafa (FiratCelik) in the summer. She loves him and wants to get married as soon as possible in order to overcome the emotional pain of grudging charity of her sister-in-law.

Anunforgettable tragedy transforms Fatmagul's life so radically that she will never be able to go back to the way she used to live. One day, she is raped by four people, Kerim (EnginAkyurek), Vural (BugraGulsoy), Erdogan (KaanTasner), and Selim (Engin Ozturk). In order to shade the sins of rapists and protect them, Fatmagul is forced to remain silent and get married to one of her rapists. Fatmagul's whole life changes after this this tragedy but bad things never end. After this tragedy, her fiancée Mustafa doesn't want to be so breaks their marriage promise.

Now, Fatmagul is alone and has no choice, but to get married to Kerim. She wants nothing more than to forgot about her checkered past and live the rest of her life quietly and at peace with the world. While she tries to start over a new life in the big city, the story becomes more complicated when her ex fiancée follows her to Istanbul?

In What is Fatmagul's Fault TV series story which is the adaptation of VedatTurkali's novel, you will explore a dramtic story of a beautiful and innocent girl. Also, this story attempts to answer whether two people – two enemies because of sins and mistakes of others – can learn to love each other in a marriage agreed only on paper. Will Mustafa catch up with Fatmagul and learn the truth? Will the rape shade the innocence? Will the past be forgotten?

Representation of women characters
Feriha:

1. Protagonist of the story.
2. Beautiful and wears rich clothes
3. Clever and Intelligent girl.
4. Lives in a luxury neighborhood.
5. Belongs to a poor family.
6. Helps parents in doing apartment chores as housekeeper.

CHARACTER ENCOUNTERING IN STORY

1. Hides the secret of being poor to her class mates.
2. Fell in love with a rich guy named Emir.
3. Struggles her identity with rich neighbors whom she worked for as house helper.
4. Faces discrimination between rich and poor status with her boyfriend and his family

Fatmagul

1. Protagonist of the story.
2. Beautiful and naïve girl.
3. Innocent and shy
4. Belongs to a poor family.

CHARACTER ENCOUNTERING IN STORY

1. Engaged to her childhood sweetheart Mustafa.
2. She gets raped by four men.
3. Mustafa breaks off their engagement.
4. Family forces her to marry one of the rapists Kerim.
5. Struggles for her dignity, innocence and justice.
6. Faces humiliation and biases of society towards male gender.

Margin to Central
Feriha

It follows housekeeper Feriha Yilmaz (Hazal Kaya), a young woman from a poor background and the daughter of Zehra Yılmaz (Vahide Percin); and Rıza Yılmaz (Metin Çekmez), a doorman. Feriha is awarded a scholarship to an elite university, where wealthy playboy Emir Sarrafoğlu (Cagatay Ulusoy) studies as well. Emir eventually falls in love with Feriha, believing she is also wealthy. Feriha is a symbol of class anxiety in Turkey; though having a university education, she is forced to lie in order to get ahead.

There, she meets a handsome and wealthy young man, Emir Sarrafoğlu (Çağatay Ulusoy), who is known for being a womanizer. Feriha lies about her life due to the fear of being rejected. She and Emir, with passing time and favorable circumstances, fall in love with each other. However, as that love grows, she becomes trapped in her own lies. Emir discovers Feriha's falsehoods and she breaks up with him. Later, Feriha is kidnapped by Halil and saved by Emir, who marries her. Both Yilmaz's and Sarrafoğlu's families get furious and break ties with them. Emir wants to protect Ece from Yavuz Sanchakter. Due to the entry of Ruia and Ece in Emir and Feriha's life, it was highly disturbing. On the day of the party, Feriha asks Emir to choose between her and work. Later, Feriha discovers Emir taking his decision. Due to a misunderstanding, Feriha divorces Emir in his absence and moves with Levent to the US for 3 years. Emir was engaged to Ece to protect her from Yavuz Sancaktar, until the problem gets solved and Feriha and Emir remarry. However, Feriha is shot by Ece on the orders of Sanem, and she dies in Emir's arms.

Fatmagul

Fatamgul is engaged to her childhood sweetheart Mustafa and is looking forward to their marriage. One night, four young men grab her and start to play around with her. They never think that the joke will turn into a rape at first. But later, they begin to rape her, one by one. The sun of her life is shadowed after that night; it's not only Fatmagul's body which was raped, but also her life. Mustafa breaks off their engagement and even worse - in order to save the honour of her family she is forced to marry one of the rapists.

"Fatmagul"'s story is of strength, justice and karma. How a rape victim turned into a powerful women? And how love can transform hate into an intimate relationship? How Fatmagul finally got justice and how she carried her life later on?

The plot revolves around a girl name Fatmagul, who lives in a village in Turkey with her brother and sister in law. Fatmagul was engaged with a local fishermen and was hoping to marry him soon.

On the night of engagement of a richest business man's son Fatmagul was working as helper to earn some money which she wanted to use later on for her wedding. Later that night she had to also see off her fiance who was going to the sea for fishing.

She decided to complete her work and get early leave so she could see off her fiance on the seashore. After the engagement ceremony the son of business man along his cousin and friends got drunk and took drugs to enjoy

They decided to go to the seashore where unfortunately Fatmagul was also heading to see off her fiance. Just when Fatmagul reached there she didn't see her fiance as he left already. She did saw four boys who were completely drunk, feeling scared she started running but was captured by the drunkards.

She was ganged raped by 3 men and one of the four man whose name was "Kerim" did not rape her. But he also didn't realize that what was happening infront of him was rape as he was drugged by his friend.

Kerim was not from a very rich background he was a local blacksmith and childhood friend of the richies who ganged rape Fatmagul.

The serial get really twisted when Kerim marry Fatmagul to protect her. Fatmagul didn't go to the police as her sister in law took money from the rapist to stay quiet.

She was suppressed to accept everything and forget her childhood love her fiance. Her fiance also left her after hearing that she was gang raped and held her responsible for everything. Fatmagul lost all hopes to get justice and eventually had to marry the man who saw her being raped by 3 men.

She started her life again after suffering from a severe trauma. She moved to Istanbul and started working as a waitress and started studying privately. She came back to life by the support of a women Maryam who found her in the woods when she was raped.

She was actually the sister of Kerim. After wedding Fatmagul couldn't accept Kerim and hated him from core. Maryam helped her recover and come back to life. With her support and love Fatmagul stood up on her feet again.

As hooks suggests, individuals who fight for the eradication of sexism without supporting struggles to end racism or classism undermine their own efforts. Individuals who fight for the eradication of racism or classism while supporting sexist oppression are helping to maintain the cultural basis of all forms of group oppression. While they may initiate successful reforms, their efforts will not lead to revolutionary change.

Like oppression stemming from sexism and racism, hooks offers an account of oppression stemming from classism. In Where we stand: class matters, hooks states that in American society, at least, "it is fashionable to talk about race or gender; the uncool subject is class. It's the subject that makes us all tense, nervous, uncertain about where we stand" (2000, 8). She claims people are scared to discuss class despite the obvious differences and conflicts between the rich and the poor since they will lose their class status once they show concern or affinity for the lower classes.

Talking of class might cause the middle class to lose their comfortable lives. However, "breaking the silence" about class is necessary to fight oppression caused by classism (hooks 2000, 8-10). She stresses, though, that class oppression is a hidden evil less readily discussed as sexism and racism.4 While it has always been obvious that some folks have more money than other folks, class difference and classism are rarely overtly apparent, or they are not acknowledged when present. Racism and sexism were easier to identify and challenge than classism. The poor have no public voice in society. No wonder it has taken so long for many citizens to recognize class— to become class conscious (hooks 2000, 14). Class is defined by hooks as,

...much more than Marx's definition of relationship to the means of production. Class involves your behavior, your basic assumptions, how you are taught to behave, what you expect from yourself and from others, your concept of a future, how you understand problems and solve them, how you think, feel, act (2009, 3).

The issue of class must first be confronted before females could unite together to fight patriarchy. Oppression by virtue of patriarchy can only be confronted if the issue of class is acknowledged. Accordingly, feminist liberation can only happen if class elitism is challenged.

All feminists should recognize the "reality of race and racism" (hooks 2000, 55). From the moment a girl is able to watch shows or films, she already finds out that black women are not always visible on screen -and a conclusion that can be made is that it is because these women are not white. All throughout hooks' cultural criticism studies, one will see the same critique of representations. She believes that all women in the United States know that "whiteness is a privileged category." The fact that white females may choose to repress or deny this knowledge does not mean they are ignorant, it may mean that they are in denial (hooks 2000, 55). If women would break free from this denial, the women's movement would be stronger. The realities of women's diversity would be exposed and "the feminist movement could face critique and challenge while still remaining wholeheartedly committed to a vision of justice, of liberation" (hooks 2000, 60).

Returning to the discussion of white supremacy, hooks claims that scholarship on women of color are biased. They attempt to show that "white girls are somehow more vulnerable to sexist conditioning than girls of color" (2000, 59). This assertion in itself can be attributed to white supremacist thinking, and she contends that the issue of race and racism be revisited by feminist thinkers. "Rarely do mainstream social critiques acknowledge this fact" (hooks 2000, 59). There is a need to further challenge the feminist movement--it should lay the foundation "for the building of a mass-based anti-racist feminist movement" (hooks 2000, 60). According to Ann Brooks, the interlocking oppressions theory would lead feminist theory to an "unsettled the normal certainties of this movement-oriented discipline and propelled it into its own distinctive sociology of knowledge (2003, 122)

Conclusion

The Girl Named Feriha Review – A Close Look Into The Turkish Drama By Talal Farooqi

The Girl Named Feriha is a widely popular Turkish series launched back in 2011. The story of the drama involves a girl named Feriha who belongs to a very poor family. As the story unfolds, she gets herself admitted to a university on the basis of a scholarship giving her a chance to excel. However, interesting turns of events take place as she is perceived rich by most of her university friends. Feriha is one of the most-watched Turkish drama series over the years. Let's have a close look into the drama to help you get started!

This drama is the story of a young, beautiful, and clever girl who lives in a luxury neighborhood but roots back to a very poor family. Feriha's father works as a maintenance guy in an apartment providing management services. Her mother also works in the same neighborhood offering cleaning services to help her father make up for a living. Feriha has a twin brother and she also helps her parents in looking after the maintenance chores. Being the only hope of the family, she struggles and gets accepted into a private university with a scholarship offer.

As the story unfolds, she becomes the center of attention among her fellow students due to her pleasant personality and the luxury clothes that she got from the neighbors. The story takes an interesting turn when one day her father arrives at her university. Feriha pretends that he is just a maintenance guy sent by her own father for some task. As soon as she speaks this lie, she gets into a series of problems that write the fate of the rest of the story.

She further claims that Friedan's theory is discriminatory as it makes the white Bourgeois woman's plight the center of feminist discourse. She also questions whether the feminist experience of white women is an adequate perspective on women's collective realities (Hooks 1984, 3). Limiting feminist theory to the discourse on gender cannot be a solid foundation for theorizing.

CHAPTER IX

Borderless Media in the age of Globalization: Its Impact on Governance and Administration

Samuel LalramdikaHnamte, Ph.D. Scholar, Department of Public Administration, Mizoram University.

Introduction

In simple terms, mass media is the means of communication through radio, television, newspapers, magazines and the internet, that reaches and influence people widely.In mass communication, media arethe communication outlets or tools used to store and deliver information.The key roles of mass media are Information, Education, Entertainment,Persuasion, Surveillance,Interpretation, Linkage,Socialization,etc.

As time passes by, the world is changing rapidly, so are its people and the technology itself. Technology brings about a lot of amendments in people's life. It is getting more advanced from day to day especially when it comes to Information Communication Technology or in this case; electronic communications. Back then, mailing was seemingly to be one of the most vital way of communication especially across the world. In contrast, nowadays people are more prone to communicate the easier ways; by staring on their electronic accounts on their computers or through their electronic gadgets like phones, ipads, laptops, etc. and sending short messages.This growing trend gives a lot of dominances in today's life, which are helping people to save their time and money, create borderless communication and make it easy for people to gain prominent information whereby creating a challenge for both the administrators as well as the governments of any country to pro-actively function.

As of today, there is no international consensus on the definition of governance.Governance addresses the exercise of political, economic and administrative authority in the management of either the world or an individual country's affairs at all levels. Governance is a concept encompassing the complex mechanisms, resources, processes and institutions by which citizens, legal entities, gender and social groups articulate their interests, mediate their differences and exercise their legal rights and duties. Governance transcends the State to include as well as the private sector, civil society and international organisations in overall development process at global, national, regional and local levels.

The media are one of the principal agents of globalisation. Their importance and power are growing, seemingly unstoppable. The World Bank recently came upon the governance-media niche indirectly through the economy. Its President gave the following explanation for this in the year 1999 i.e "What became very clear to me was that the issue of corruption and the issue of press freedom, while they may have political impact, are in fact essential issues in terms of economic development. Any movement for equity, social justice and corruption needs a free press for it to work." That was how the World Bank convinced itself that the fight against corruption, the aspiration to greater transparency in the management and functioning of the apparatus of State, and the need to account to the people have become democratic requirements, indispensable for economic development but difficult to achieve without the intermediation of the media.

Freedom of expression is regarded as the foremost of the individual freedoms. Without it, all the other freedoms would be unable to endure for long. It is the essential basis of the democratic State. Freedom of the press in the broad sense (written and audiovisual press) and more generally freedom of communication (including the new media) are the corollaries of freedom of expression. Freedom of expression is a right embodied in the Universal Declaration of Human Rights (Article 19) and also in the International Covenant on Civil and Political Rights (Article 19). Where the rule of law does not exist, or exists only partially, the media, no matter how imperfect they may be, should nevertheless be encouraged. It is often they who pave the way for freedom and democracy. Freedom of expression, in all countries and in all cultures, is an ideal that never exists in its pure state; in reality it is approached more or less well through fragile consensus, delicate compromise, setbacks and temporary victories. The media, the principal vehicle for freedom of expression, are therefore at the very heart of the problem of governance: they navigate within legal frameworks, more or less sympathetic to freedom of expression; they organise themselves in defense of their credibility (codes of ethics, self-regulation); they make more or less proper use of their margin of freedom to address a society on the move, and they take part in campaigns in support of governance. The pre-eminence of freedom of expression among other individual freedoms is not without a degree of ambiguity for the media. A newspaper that publishes full pages on human rights (possibly in collaboration with NGOs) might also remain silent on certain issues, or may be corrupt. A national radio station may stir up local conflicts, in the belief that it is providing information in the general interest. Conversely, local radio stations save lives every day by defusing conflicts about which the outside world knows nothing. Because of this, international cooperation makes more and more use of the media in projects to prevent conflict and to inform in a period of political crisis or natural disaster. Despite these ambiguities,is working on the media to realise the objectives of participation, gender balanced development, transparency, respect for the rule of law and the emergence of a civil society.

Every medium has its own special characteristics. Some media are better suited to development operations than others. The degree of freedom they enjoy is different, too. Depending on the goals they are pursuing and the public they are addressing, we can count on one or another, or even on a measured combination. The popular forms of mass media are as follows:

1. Traditional communication –Societies did not have to wait for the flood of modern media in order to communicate. Even today, the most powerful medium is still word of mouth. Information spread by the mass media doesn't survive for long if it isn't picked up, discussed and commented on in the street.

2. Radio - This is the most popular medium, and often the most appropriate for development. It is not necessary to be able to read and write, live in towns or be rich to benefit from it. It is all the more effective because it is a direct continuation of oral culture. Two fairly recent developments have made radio a particularly interesting medium from the point of view of governance, especially for participation and decentralisation. Broadcasting on FM wavelengths, which enables many different local radio stations to be set up, well suited for participation and interaction. The emergence of radio pluralism in many countries tied to the past by an audiovisual monopoly.

3. Press agencies - Their function is to supply raw information rapidly to the media that the latter will then complete, synthesise and comment on. In poor countries, editors often don't have the means to subscribe to the national Press Agency, even if it is subsidised. In such cases, agencies are reduced to producing a simple bulletin that they print and sell like a

newspaper.

4. Newspapers- This is an essentially urban medium. Illiteracy, the high cost of paper, low advertising revenue and distribution problems are the main obstacles to their circulation nationally. Their precarious economic situation also sometimes leads them to yield to economic or political pressures. For all that, they play a strategic role in forming the opinions of the elite, in democratic interaction, and in exposing abuses. The written press is growing strongly in Asia, but declining in South America and in jeopardy in Africa and Eastern Europe.

5. Television - This is the medium of the collective imagination. Images of major football matches, series from Brazil, Mexico and the USA give the whole world something to dream about, and not understanding the language is no obstacle. The future of television will be more democratic, simpler technology will soon enable it to be decentralised and participative – like radio.

The new media (Internet, e-mail, mobile phones) is a sector that is really buzzing and evolving rapidly. The new media carry great hopes for countries where SDC is active. At the same time, their technical requirements (modern telecommunications infrastructures, the ability to read and write and mastery of the keyboard and the mouse) are a new obstacle to the participation of many citizens in the global information society. Overcoming the digital divide therefore poses a new challenge, one that international cooperation has to take up. The potential of the new media for governance (more transparency, more democracy, more consultation, more information, etc.) is enormous. But there is a growing trend among States, no matter how liberal, to control them. In terms of governance, we must emphasise that the new media favour networks, overcome distances and strengthen horizontal communication and civil society organisations; reduce the effects of isolation; facilitate decentralization,etc.

There are some notable exceptions, but overall, development actors spend relatively small sums on media support, often not investing for the long term and struggling to integrate the media into broader policy agendas. When they do, it is usually with the aim of achieving one (or more) of the following objectives:

- Democracy and human rights: To build an independent media sector as an intrinsic good, essential to the functioning of a democratic society and a key platform for freedom of expression.
- Accountability: To enhance the accountability of governments to citizens, often in order to: improve service delivery, state responsiveness and state-citizen relations; support more informed democratic/electoral decision-making or marginalised groups to assert their voice; or decrease public tolerance of corruption or poor governance.
- Stability and conflict reduction: To improve debate, dialogue and tolerance in fragile or conflict-affected societies, often in order to: increase the availability of balanced, reliable and trustworthy information; reduce the likelihood of hate speech or inflammatory media likely to exacerbate conflict; and enhance social cohesion or build state legitimacy.
- Communication for development: To create demand for services and use the media as an instrument to shift behaviour or change the social norms that prevent such behaviour. For example, improving immunisation uptake.

Responsibility of Media in POLITICO-ADMINISITRATION

- Media aims to supply relevant, genuine, and fair information to the citizens without any discrepancies, misinformation, or manipulation.
- In developing democratic counties, the media plays a role as a mode of reducing the illiteracy rate.
- Through the media, the citizens would get details on what is happening in the world around them. It prompts me to think about the conditions and get an education on different parameters.
- The citizens can reside in better harmony and better understand their judicial services.
- The role of media in democracy-based countries is to showcase issues that affect economic, political, and social liberty to the public.

Benefits of Social Media for Governments (POLITICO-ADMINISTRATION)

In the context of the role of media in society, digital media is the current form of preferred medium. Social media i.e. FACEBOOK, WHATS APP, TWITTER, INSTAGRAM, URKUND, etc. is a powerful tool for managing and shifting public sentiments and information management among the different types. So, governments depend on social media highly currently for public interaction and administration. There are multiple reasons for the government's increasing usage of social media.

Communication about Crisis

Through social media platforms, the governments of different countries can communicate information about major crises directly to the public. The ones in power use this medium to soften the tensions of their citizens and provide the necessary updates.

The public turns to the message boards and social media posts from authorized personnel for crisis-related information. Plus, governments can communicate what they are doing for prevention, safety, and maintenance.

Information about True News

Through social media, governmental organizations can address concerns and misinformation fast, especially in times of panic. They can detect and mention the inaccuracies in wrong sources and avoid false information spreading.

Engagement with Citizens

One major role of the media in the government is to increase engagement between the central power and the citizens. With personalized and informative content on display about the issues and policies, the public trust can grow.

Cost-saving

Instead of the conventional public outreach methods, social media-based information exchanges cost less. So, governmental agencies adopt this to reduce advertising and public relations expenses.

Media is an effective medium for showcasing important information about global matters, entertainment, and government policies to the public. The role of the media is to inform citizens on facts with no distortion of the truth.

The media works on the side of the public to ask the important questions to the ones in power and reports ongoing injustices and issues.

Governments in democracies depend highly on the media to strengthen their public engagement and administrative functionality. Therefore, they use the power of media types like social media to inform the public on facts and crisis alerts quickly.

The evolution of media is a fascinating journey. Print media was responsible for conveying information regarding freedom struggle of great leaders. It continues to remain popular despite fierce competition and is still the preferred medium for reaching out to masses as wellas classes.

On the other hand, the Radio is a simple medium that is portable as well. Radio wields its influence greatly in rural areas where a majority may not know how to read or write. Since a large chunk of the population is still illiterate, this medium is critical for government as well who would like to communicate any urgent information such as weatherrelated warnings.

Television is a phenomenon that continues to grab the maximum eyeballs. It's a well established fact that visual medium does have the greatest impact. The presentation and the catchy visuals do ensure that a large part of the country is tuned in for entertainment as well as information. The latest medium is the Internet that combines the audio and visual effects to reach out to millions of users worldwide. Unlike television or radio, one can just look at the internet at a convenient time. The power of social media and internet is now rife, which is the reason that the government is now increasingly focusing on the internet to reach out to a large section of the youth.

Why Media is particularly important for India?

Since good governance comprises of accountability, transparent, responsive, equitable and inclusive as well as effective and efficient, Media has a huge role in ensuring that all of these criteria are met from time to time. Good governance essentially means how public institutions conduct public affairs and manage public resources.

For a developing country like India which still reels with superstition, communalism and casteism, the involvement of media becomes even more important. The backward and ignorance of poor should make the media emboldened regarding their responsibility to bring them modern ideas for eliminating poverty and other social evils.

Another reason why media is of paramount importance for the country is because of the immense disparity that is prevalent. Despite being one of the fastest growing economies of the world, it is ranked pathetically lower than even its neighbours in the Human Development Index. While a large number of journalists cover the more glamourous and glitzy events and news, less report on the number of deaths or the unemployment scenario. The rationality of media lies in helping the government fight diseases such as AIDS, Polio, Cancer along with promoting latest technologies for the development of its citizens.

Media should be vigilant about the laws of the country and that they are not violated by institutions of the government or any other rogue elements. In this aspect, it has demonstrated its excellence in bringing to book some of the law breakers in recent times. In fact, it has gone an extra mile by putting pressure to ensure that justice is given to victims. However, often we find that it surpasses its role of a watchdog and instead attempts to give the verdict, which is the Judiciary's responsibility.

A lot of governments across the world have faced charges of corruption highlighted by media and that has often led to either overthrowing of corrupt administration or bringing in more transparency into the system. Hence, the fourth estate can help in efficacy to the existing scheme of things as well.

One of the strongest roles of media is that it tries to engage millions of viewers, listeners or readers. In this manner, the fundamental role of ensuring participation of its citizens in the decision making process of the country is done by media very well.

Conclusion

The role of media has risen over the time and it would gain more importance in the times to come as many across the world still yearn for better governance or at best governance itself and not autocratic rule. While media does highlight some of the concerns from time to time, it does not delve deeper into the real issues. The checks and balances which media ensures by reporting issues in an objective manner can go a long way in ensuring that governance by government would be fair and fruitful.

The Bottom Line is that if any form of government aims to enhance transparency and accountability in its functioning, sharing pivotal information with the community has to top the list of priorities. Making information speedy and simple to find and at the same time, getting the whole area (maybe city,village,etc.) on the same page will go a long way in promoting trust and faith, demonstrating integrity, and nurturing confidence in the government.

Reference:

1. Deane, James (2013), "Fragile states: The role of media and communication", Policy Briefing, No. 10, BBC Media Action.
2. Dr Nilanchala Sethy, (2017), "Press and Media Law: Its Impact on the Administration of Justice".

3. Francis Philip (2021), "Social Media in India: Regulatory Needs, Issues and Challenges"

4. John Pierrie, (2019), "Media and Governance: Exploring the Role of News Media in Complex Systems of Governance (New Perspectives in Policy and Politics)".

5. Ministry of Administrative Reform & e-Government (2014), Greek Action Plan 2014-2016.

6. Media Regulation: Governance and the Interests of Citizens and Consumers.

7. Shanti Kalanti (2011),"A Toolkit for Independent Media Development".